HRW READING

READING TODAY AND TOMORROW

PATHWAYS

LEVEL 8

Isabel L. Beck, Senior Author

Lenore H. Ringler
Donna M. Ogle
Taffy E. Raphael
Bonnie B. Armbruster
Margaret G. McKeown

HOLT, RINEHART AND WINSTON, INC.
Austin New York Chicago San Diego Toronto Montreal

Permissions
Holt, Rinehart and Winston, Inc.
1627 Woodland Drive
Austin, Texas 78741

Printed in the United States of America
ISBN 0-15-718070-0
89012 061 7654321A

Acknowledgments

For permission to reprint copyrighted material, grateful acknowledgment is made to the following sources:

Carnival Press, Inc.: Adaptation of *Angel Child, Dragon Child* by Michele Maria Surat. Copyright © 1983 by Carnival Press, Inc.

Dial Books for Young Readers: Adaptation of "Mr. Rabbit and Mr. Bear" from *The Knee-High Man and Other Tales* by Julius Lester with illustrations by Ralph Pinto. Copyright © 1972 by Julius Lester; illustrations copyright © 1972 by Ralph Pinto.

Farrar, Straus & Giroux, Inc.: Adaptation of *To Hilda for Helping* by Margot Zemach. Text and illustrations copyright © 1977 by Margot Zemach.

Aileen Fisher: "Hideout" from *In the Woods, In the Meadow, In the Sky* by Aileen Fisher. Copyright © 1965 by Aileen Fisher.

Greenwillow Books, a division of William Morrow, Inc.: Adaptation of *Old Turtle's Baseball Stories* written and illustrated by Leonard Kessler. Copyright © 1982 by Leonard Kessler.

Harcourt Brace Jovanovich, Inc.: Abridged and adapted from *Jane Martin, Dog Detective*. Copyright © 1984 by Eve Bunting. Abridged and adapted from *Gabrielle and Selena* by Peter Desbarats. Copyright © 1968 by Peter Desbarats.

Harper & Row, Publishers, Inc.: "The Giant" from *All That Sunlight* by Charlotte Zolotow. Copyright © 1967 by Charlotte Zolotow. Adaptation of *Through Grandpa's Eyes* by Patricia MacLachlan. Illustrated by Deborah Ray. Text copyright © 1979 by Patricia MacLachlan; illustrations copyright © 1980 by Ray Studios, Inc. Adaptation and abridgment of *Thanksgiving at the Tappletons'* by Eileen Spinelli. Copyright © 1982 by Eileen Spinelli.

Houghton Mifflin Company: Adaptation of *Fritz and the Beautiful Horses* by Jan Brett. Copyright © 1981 by Jan Brett. "Why the Sky Is Blue" from *Fast and Slow* by John Ciardi. Copyright © 1975 by John Ciardi. Adaptation of *Why the Sun and the Moon Live in the Sky* by Elphinstone Dayrell and illustrated by Blair Lent. Copyright © 1968 by Blair Lent, Jr.

Alfred A. Knopf, Inc.: "Poem" ("I Loved My Friend") from *The Dream Keeper and Other Poems* by Langston Hughes. Copyright © 1932 by Alfred A. Knopf and renewed 1960 by Langston Hughes. Excerpt from "The Octopus" from *A Child's Bestiary* by John Gardner. Copyright © 1977 by Boskydell Artists, Ltd.

(continued on page 296)

LEVEL 8

Contents

1 Families

2 Something's Missing

3 A Different Way

4 Making Plans

PATHWAYS

UNIT 1

FAMILIES

There are all kinds of families . . . families of people and families of animals . . . families that care and families that share. Each story in this unit is about a family.

In the first story, you'll read about a family that learns the real meaning of Thanksgiving. Then you'll find out about a surprise an uncle has for his family. You'll also read a selection about a special baby animal and how it grows. In another story, a girl is unhappy because of something her sister has. In an old tale, something very funny happens when a man asks a favor of his family. And, in the last story, a boy tries to "see" things in the special way that his grandfather does.

As you read the stories in this unit, think about the families you are getting to know. How do the members of each family treat one another? What kinds of things do they learn from each other?

The Tappleton family is getting ready for Thanksgiving. What will make this Thanksgiving different?

Thanksgiving at the Tappletons'

by Eileen Spinelli

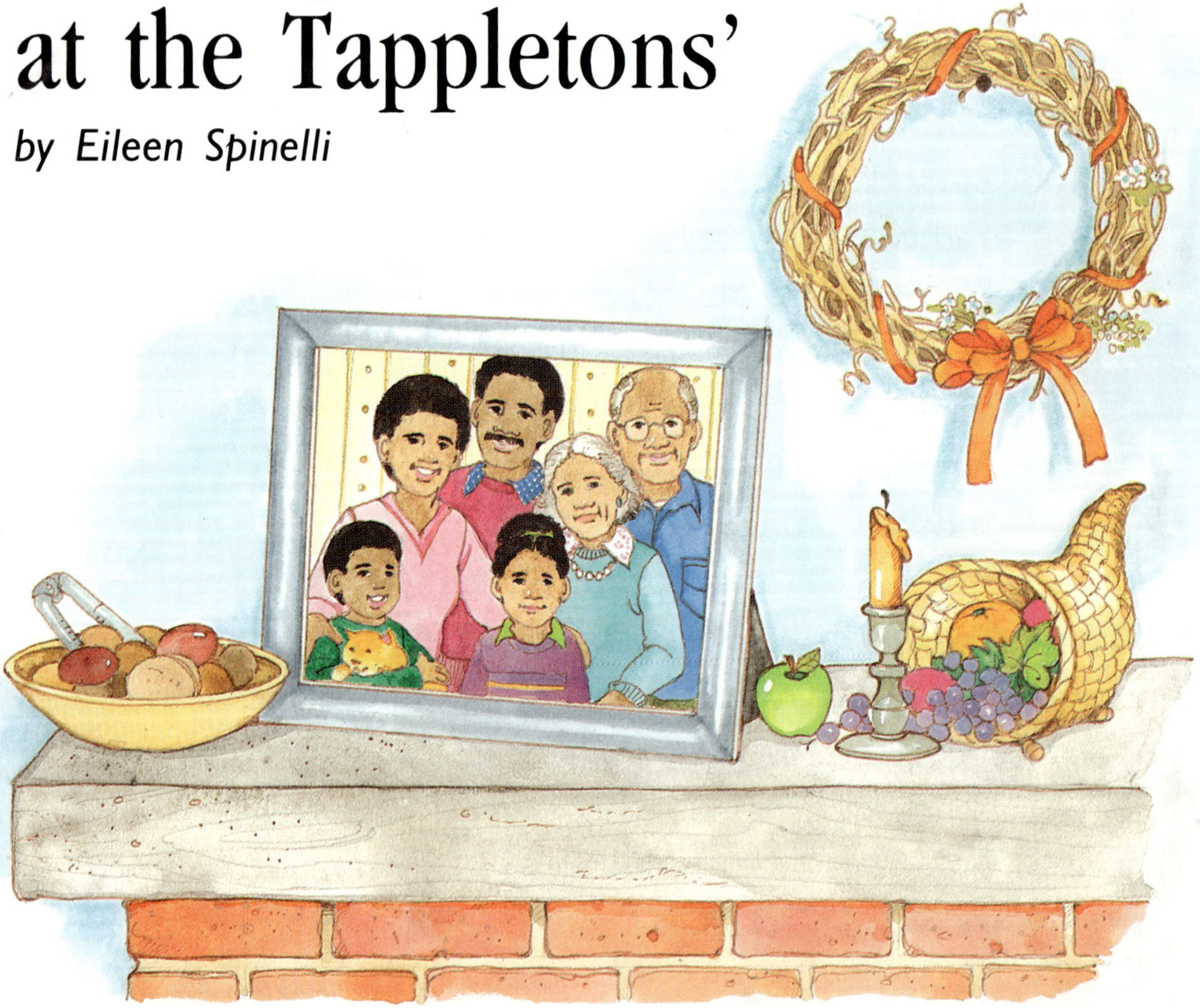

Thanksgiving at the Tappletons' was always a big day. Thanksgiving at the Tappletons' meant the family would be together. And, of course, Thanksgiving at the Tappletons' meant the turkey with all the trimmings.

One Thanksgiving morning, Mrs. Tappleton was up before sunrise. She lit the oven and took the big turkey out of the refrigerator. Just then Mike, the milkman, tapped on the kitchen door.

"Good morning, Mrs. Tappleton," he said. "I thought you'd like some eggnog for your dinner."

As Mrs. Tappleton reached for the eggnog, the turkey slipped from under her arm. Now on a warmer day this probably wouldn't have been a problem, but today the step was covered with ice. Before she or Mike could even think, the turkey had slithered into the yard.

"Stop that turkey!" yelled Mrs. Tappleton. Mike reached out, but the turkey skidded past him. It slid down the hill and into the pond.

Plop! Splash! The turkey was gone.

When Mr. Tappleton came downstairs later, he stood and took a long sniff. "I don't smell turkey," he said to his wife.

"You don't smell turkey because you have a cold," she said.

"I don't have a cold," he insisted.

Mrs. Tappleton shook some pepper in the air. Mr. Tappleton sneezed. "See," she said, "you *do* have a cold."

Then she called to her son, "Kenny, you may make the salad today. The vegetables are in the refrigerator."

Kenny's face grew pale. Just yesterday he had fed all the vegetables to the rabbits in Mr. Cook's class. He couldn't tell his mother. So he covered the empty salad bowl with foil and stuck the bowl in the refrigerator.

Later, everyone but Jenny went to the train to pick up Grandmother and Grandfather Tappleton. Jenny stayed home to make the mashed potatoes.

Just as Jenny turned on the mixer, the telephone rang. It was her friend, Nora. Jenny talked and talked, and she would still be talking today had not a wet glump of something hit her on the head. Jenny turned to see what it was. Mashed potatoes were flying everywhere.

Jenny quickly hung up the telephone and wiped mashed potatoes from nearly everything in the kitchen. She finished just as the others came back.

As Grandfather Tappleton came through the door, he said, "I'm as hungry as an elephant."

Everyone sat down at the table.

"I'll carve the turkey now," said Mr. Tappleton. He opened the oven door. "The turkey is gone!"

Mrs. Tappleton took a deep breath. She explained to them how the fine turkey had slipped out the door and—plop! splash!—into the pond.

"So much for the turkey," said Mr. Tappleton.

"We can fill up on the trimmings," said Grandmother.

"I'll get the salad," Jenny said. When she pulled off the foil, everyone stared at the salad that was not there.

"I fed the rabbits at school," confessed Kenny.

"So much for the salad," said Mr. Tappleton.

"I'm as hungry as *two* elephants," said Grandfather, looking very gloomy.

Kenny jumped up. "We'll have Jenny's mashed potatoes." He went and got the pot from the kitchen and lifted the lid.

"The mixer went crazy," said Jenny.

"So much for the potatoes," said Mr. Tappleton.

"*Three* elephants," groaned Grandfather.

Everyone looked at the empty table.

"No Thanksgiving dinner," sniffed Jenny.

"Nothing to say thanks for," muttered Kenny.

"Of course there is!" said Grandmother, smiling. "Thanksgiving is more than just turkey and trimmings."

Grandmother asked everyone to join hands. And this is what she said:

Turkeys come and turkeys go
And trimmings can be lost, we know.
But we're together, that's what matters—
Not what's served upon the platters.

"How wonderful!" said Grandfather.

Mrs. Tappleton jumped up. "We have ham and cheese in the refrigerator."

"I'll help fix the sandwiches," offered Mr. Tappleton.

"I'll get the pickles," said Jenny.

Kenny laughed. "I'll open a can of corn."

So the Tappletons had their Thanksgiving dinner after all. Grandfather ate as much as *four* elephants. In fact, *everyone* had plenty to eat. Best of all, they had each other.

Discussing the Selection

1. What made this Thanksgiving different for the Tappletons?
2. What happened to the turkey and the trimmings?
3. What happened when the family first sat down to eat dinner?
4. Find and read the part in the story where you learned what Thanksgiving really meant to the Tappletons.
5. What do you think the Tappletons talked about as they ate their dinner?

Using Language

Writing About Thanksgiving

Prewriting The Tappletons had an extra-special Thanksgiving Day. Think what made their Thanksgiving so special. What do you think the Tappletons learned on that Thanksgiving day?

Writing Pretend that you are Jenny or Kenny Tappleton. Write a story about your Thanksgiving and what made it special. Tell about things that happened to the Tappletons to make your story seem like Jenny or Kenny wrote it.

Postwriting Trade papers with a friend and read each other's stories. Tell your friend what you like best about his or her story.

Painting Pictures With Words

Sometimes, when you read a good story, you can picture the people and places the author is describing. The better the author's description is, the clearer the picture becomes.

Read the following sentences from "Thanksgiving at the Tappletons' ":

1. Before Mrs. Tappleton or Mike could even think, the turkey had slithered into the yard.
2. Mike reached out, but the turkey skidded past him.
3. Plop! Splash! The turkey was gone.

The author probably could have said what happened to the turkey in a single sentence, such as "Mrs. Tappleton dropped the turkey, and it fell into the pond."

Instead, the author used descriptive words like *slithered*, *skidded*, and *plop* to give readers a better picture of what happened. You can just see Mrs. Tappleton and Mike sliding down the icy hill after the runaway turkey. In this case, the descriptive words also added humor to the story. Now read the following sentences:

1. I saw a parachute in the sky.
2. I saw a balloon-shaped parachute drifting gently across the sky.

The first sentence tells a fact—someone saw a parachute in the sky. The second sentence tells the same fact, but with more descriptive words. Which sentence is more interesting to you? Why?

Descriptive words can spark a reader's interest. When you write something, try to use descriptive words so your readers can picture what you are describing.

(To be read by the teacher)

Uncles

Uncles are brothers to fathers;
Uncles are brothers to mothers;
Uncles are fathers to cousins, of course,
And related to various others.
Uncles are husbands to aunts.
And I'm happy they happen to be;
But the very best thing about uncles, I think,
Is that uncles are uncles to me!

Mary Ann Hoberman

Paco always enjoys his uncle's visits. Read to find out what makes this visit different.

Tío Roberto's Visit

by Florence Parry Heide and Roxanne Heide Pierce

"It's so hard to wait," Paco said, hopping up and down the steps.

Papa laughed. "It's always so hard for *you* to wait. Every summer before Tío Roberto comes to visit, you hop and jump around like a little monkey."

Paco made a funny face and monkey sounds. What Papa said was right—it was always hard to wait. And Paco loved his uncle's visits.

"Saturday will never come," groaned Paco.

"It will come," said Mama. "You'll see."

"It will come," said Papa. "Trust your mother. I always do."

Two days before Tío was to arrive, a letter came for Paco. Paco opened the letter and started to read it to Mama.

Dear Paco,
I will be there on Saturday. I'm bringing Elena with me.

Paco looked up. "Elena! Who's Elena?"

Mama shrugged and said, "I don't know. Read on."

Paco looked back at the letter.

I am in love with Elena.

Mama smiled a big smile. "Tío Roberto in love! Imagine that!"

Paco felt his heart sinking. He kept reading.

I hope you will love her as much as I do. See you soon.
Love,
Tío Roberto

"Oh, no!" cried Paco. "This Elena's going to spoil everything. Why does Tío Roberto have to bring her here?"

"This Elena must be very nice," said Mama. "If Tío loves her, we will *all* love her."

"I won't like her," grumbled Paco.

"You will like her," said Mama. "Your heart will make room."

"You will like her," said Papa. "Trust your mother."

"But Tío and I always go for drives in his little red sports car," said Paco. "There's only room for the two of us."

"So you'll do something else," said Papa.

"And we always go fishing in that little boat," said Paco. "There's only room for Tío and me."

Suddenly he wanted to be alone. He put the letter down and started to walk to his room. "I'm not going to like her, and I'm not going to like Tío's visit if she's coming," he declared.

"We'll just wait and see," said Mama.

Saturday came. Paco sat on the steps feeling glum. He was going to be happy to see Tío again, but nothing would be the same. The little red sports car would be coming soon. Elena would be sitting where Paco was supposed to sit. He began to wonder what she would be like. Would she be as much fun as Tío Roberto?

"No way!" he said to himself. "She's going to spoil everything!"

Just then Tío's car pulled up in front of the house. Out jumped Tío. Out jumped a little dog with its tail wagging.

"This is Elena," said Tío. "She's a wonderful dog, and I love her."

Paco couldn't stop smiling. Now he understood. "I love her, too," he said.

"Woof! Woof!" barked Elena.

"Do you think we can still have a good time?" asked Tío with a twinkle in his eye.

"You bet," said Paco.

Discussing the Selection

1. What made this visit from Tío Roberto different?
2. Why wasn't Paco looking forward to this visit?
3. Why do you think Tío Roberto sent a letter to Paco?
4. Find and read the part where Paco changed his mind about Elena.
5. How do you think Paco would have acted if Elena had been a person?

Using Language

Writing a New Ending

Prewriting Think of other ways that the story could have ended. What if Elena had been a person instead of a dog? Would Paco have grown to like her? Jot down some ideas for a new story ending, beginning with the part of the story when Tío Roberto arrived.

Writing Write your new story ending. How would Paco have acted if Elena had been a person? What would Mama and Papa have said? What might Paco, Tío, and Elena have done together?

Postwriting Trade papers with a classmate. How are your endings alike? How are they different?

A baby dolphin named Spray was born in a tank in Florida. What did people learn about dolphins by watching Spray grow?

The Story of Spray

by Margaret Davidson

One spring morning in 1947, a man stood by a tank at Marine Studios in Florida. He leaned over and stared at one of the dolphins. Then he turned and yelled, "Come quick! Mona had her baby!"

People came running from all directions. For the first time, a baby dolphin had been born in a tank. This meant that the people at Marine Studios were going to have the chance to study a dolphin from birth.

People weren't the only ones interested in the birth. The other dolphins in the tank had formed a tight circle around Mona. Perhaps they were curious, too, but they had another reason for gathering around.

Dolphins do not have enemies in the tank, but they do have enemies in the sea. Killer whales are their enemies, and so are sharks. A newborn dolphin is only three feet long. It would make a very tasty snack for a hungry whale or shark. So the other dolphins gathered around to protect the baby.

As soon as Spray, the baby dolphin, entered the water, she had a job to do. She had to swim to the top of the tank for her first breath of air. Spray quickly wriggled her tail and got to the top of the tank by herself.

People later learned that sometimes a baby dolphin is too weak to make that first swim by itself. Or it swims in the wrong direction—down! But the mother dolphin is always right there to help her baby.

Some animals are almost helpless when they are born. Dolphins are different. From the very first, Spray could see, hear, and swim. In addition, she could "talk" to her mother. The little dolphin made a whistling noise through her blowhole, and Mona whistled right back.

Spray could do some of the things that big dolphins do, but she couldn't eat fish. She had no teeth, but that was all right because she didn't need them yet. For many months, she would drink her mother's milk.

One day, Spray found a piece of fish in the water, and she swallowed it by mistake. Poor Spray! She was still too little to eat fish. It was plain that Spray didn't feel well, but Mona knew just what to do. She rubbed and rubbed Spray's belly with her flipper. Finally, Spray gave a little burp and felt better again.

Spray ate underwater, and she slept there, too, but she could never sleep for very long. She had to come up for air, so she took catnaps instead. Sometimes Spray would close both eyes when she slept, but often she would sleep with only one eye closed—the one on the outside. She kept her other eye wide open, so she could watch her mother.

Mona kept an eye on Spray, too. At first, this was easy because Spray stuck to her mother's side like a small shadow. But as the weeks passed, Spray grew bigger and braver. She would swim farther and farther away from her mother. Mona would have to swim after Spray and bring her back—again and again.

But, finally, Mona got upset with Spray for swimming away. To punish her, Mona pushed Spray down to the bottom of the tank. Then she sat on Spray and held her in that position!

Did the punishment work? It certainly did! For a long time after that, Spray was a *very* quiet, *very* well-behaved dolphin.

Mona was a careful mother, but she seemed to know when to let Spray start taking care of herself. By the time Spray was six months old, she had teeth. Spray could now eat fish without getting sick.

By the time Spray was a year old, she was almost full-grown. It was time for Spray to live on her own, but often she would swim right back to Mona's side. Spray and her mother would always be the best of friends.

Discussing the Selection

1. What did people learn about dolphins by watching Spray grow?
2. How did Spray and Mona "talk"?
3. What did the other dolphins do that showed they were like a family?
4. Tío Roberto had a new pet that was special to him. What was special about the birth of Spray to the people at Marine Studios?

Using Language

Asking Questions

Planning Get together with a friend. One of you pretend to be a reporter covering the story of the birth of Spray. One of you pretend to be a person who trains and feeds the dolphins at Marine Studios.

Working Together Make up a set of questions the reporter can ask the trainer. The reporter may want to ask when and where the birth happened and why it was such big news. The trainer will answer the questions about the birth of Spray.

Sharing Have the reporter ask the trainer some questions in front of the class.

Two sisters have a disagreement.
Read to find out why.

To Hilda for Helping

Adapted from the book by Margot Zemach

Every night when it was dinnertime, Gladys and Rose found lots of things to do. Hilda always set the table, and she didn't complain.

One day, her father said she should have a medal for helping. So he made one for her out of a tin-can top. On the medal he wrote: TO HILDA FOR HELPING. A safety pin was attached to the back.

Hilda wore the medal all the time. She pinned it on her coat, on her shirt, and on her bathrobe. Rose didn't care about Hilda's medal, but it made Gladys mad. Every time she saw the medal, it made her madder.

Sometimes Gladys would holler at Hilda. Sometimes she would fight with her, and sometimes Gladys wouldn't let Hilda use any of her things.

Hilda had a secret. The secret was that Gladys was jealous because of the medal.

One morning, Hilda had the medal pinned to her pajamas. Gladys was feeling really mad, so she said, "Someday you're going to lose that nasty old medal. In the summertime, you'll take it outside, and you'll drop it.

"The medal will get dirty, and the rain will rain on it and make it rusty. People passing will step on your medal and kick it out of sight. It will get buried in the roots of a tree, and you'll forget all about your medal for years and years.

"When you are older, you'll come along and see something sticking out of the dirt. You'll kick it with your shoe.

" 'What's this?' you'll say. It will be your medal, all bent up and filthy. The words will be worn off so nobody, not even you, can read what they say."

"No, that's *not* what will happen!" said Hilda. "If I do take the medal outside in the summertime, and if I drop it in the dirt, maybe a little dog will find it shining in the moonlight. Maybe that dog will bury it deep under the roots of a tree.

"The rain will come down and water the tree. The tree will grow and grow. Someday leaves will come on the branches, and the leaves will all be medals!

"When I am older and I am passing by, I'll look up and see all the medals. They will be shining brightly in the sunlight so I can read what they say:

"TO HILDA FOR HELPING!"

Discussing the Selection

1. Why did the girls disagree?
2. How did Gladys feel about Hilda's medal?
3. What did Gladys say would happen to Hilda's medal?
4. What did Hilda say would happen?
5. How would you have felt about Hilda's medal if you had been Gladys?

Using Language

Making Medals

Prewriting Hilda's father made a medal for Hilda because she was helpful. Think of someone who you think should have a medal.

Writing List some reasons why the person should have a medal. Think of what you would say if you were to give the medal to the person. Make a medal using a paper plate, ribbon, lace, markers, and anything else you think would look nice.

Postwriting If you would like, give the medal to the person and tell why you made it.

Hasan asks some members of his family to do him a favor. What will they say?

New Patches for Old

by Barbara K. Walker

One day, Hasan the Shoemaker closed his shop for the afternoon.

"Tomorrow night the holidays begin," he said. "I'll buy some new things for my family."

For his wife, Hasan got a jacket. For his mother, he got a knitted scarf. For his married daughter, he got four bright hair ribbons.

Then, looking down at his own clothes, he said, "I must buy a new pair of trousers for myself. These old ones are just patches on patches."

Hasan hurried to the tailor's shop. "Have you trousers to fit me?" Hasan asked the tailor.

"See for yourself," said the tailor. "I have only one pair left."

Hasan held that pair up to himself. "They seem all right around the waist," he said, "but they're three fingers too long. Can you shorten them?"

"Not today," said the tailor. "Ask your wife to shorten them."

"All right," said Hasan, so he paid the tailor and hurried home.

Hasan's wife liked her jacket. "How fine!" she said. "And what did you buy for yourself?"

"These trousers, but they're three fingers too long," he said. "Could you shorten them?"

"Not now," said his wife. "I want to sew some beads on my new jacket. Why not ask your mother?"

Hasan went to his mother's house. "Mother," he said, "I got you a new scarf for the holidays."

"How fine!" said his mother. "And what did you buy for yourself?"

"These trousers, but they're three fingers too long," he said. "Could you shorten them?"

"I have no time to sew now," said his mother. "I must bake some breads. Why not ask your daughter?"

So Hasan went to his daughter's house. "Daughter," he said, "I got you some ribbons for the holidays."

"How fine!" said his daughter. "And what did you buy for yourself?"

"These trousers, but they're three fingers too long," he said. "Could you shorten them?"

"Not now," said his daughter. "I must feed the baby. Surely Mother will shorten them."

Hasan thought and thought. Then he hurried back to his shop.

He cut a piece three fingers wide from the end of each trouser leg. With his big shoemaker's needle, he put new hems in the trousers. Then, putting them over his arm, he went along home and put them on his shelf.

The next afternoon, Hasan closed his shop and went home. His wife met him at the door. "Come in," she said. "Your mother and our daughter are here."

Hasan's mother looked lovely in her new scarf. "As soon as you're ready, Son," she said, "we'll all go to the holiday festival." Then Hasan's mother smiled, for she had a secret.

"Husband, do be quick," said Hasan's wife. "Put on those new trousers. I am wearing my new jacket." Hasan's wife was smiling, for she had a fine secret.

"Please, Father, don't be long," said Hasan's daughter, with her new ribbons blooming in her hair. Hasan's daughter was smiling about a secret of her own.

Hasan went into the bedroom to put on his new trousers, trousers exactly right around the waist *and* exactly the right length. He should know, for hadn't he shortened them himself?

"Oh, no!" cried Hasan. "Something has happened to my trousers!" And, opening the door, he stood there to show what he meant. His fine new trousers were no longer than knickers. They hung just below his knees.

Hasan's wife, Hasan's mother, and Hasan's daughter all said, "But I shortened them only three fingers!"

Then they guessed what must have happened. They stared at Hasan. Hasan stared back at them, too stunned to speak.

Hasan looked from his wife, to his mother, to his daughter. Then he laughed and said, "But I had already shortened them myself!"

"You!" they exclaimed. "We wish we had known!"

"Someone had to do it," said Hasan, "so I cut off the ends and hemmed them up myself."

Suddenly, they all started to laugh. In the middle of their laughing, Hasan's wife, his mother, and his daughter thought of what they could do. They could take the pieces they had cut from the trousers and sew them back on . . . which is just what they did.

When they had finished, the trousers were just the right length.

"Well, my dears," said Hasan, "at least all my patches are *new* patches!"

And, dressed in their holiday finery, away they all went to the festival.

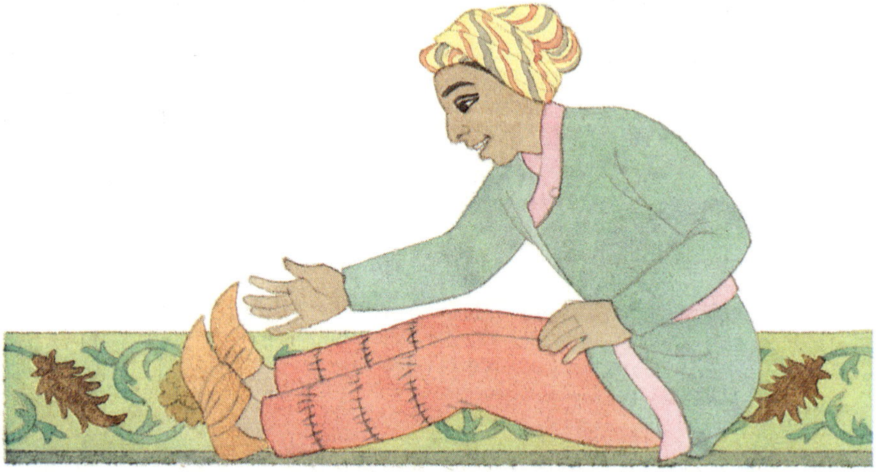

Discussing the Selection

1. What did Hasan's family say when he asked them to shorten his trousers?
2. Why did Hasan buy trousers that were too long for him?
3. What happened when Hasan dressed for the festival?
4. When did you first know that the three women had each hemmed the trousers? Find that part of the story.
5. If you had been Hasan, would you have been happy with new trousers with new patches? Why or why not?

Using Language

Meeting a Friend

Planning Pretend that Hasan meets a friend at the festival who knows that Hasan has gotten new trousers. The friend looks surprised to see Hasan in trousers with patches.

Working Together Get together with a friend. One of you pretend to be Hasan and the other pretend to be his friend. Make up some things the two friends might say to each other at the festival.

Sharing Have Hasan and his friend talk in front of the class.

DECODING/
VOCABULARY SKILL

Words That Sound Alike

Some words sound alike but have different spellings and meanings. Read the following sentence:

> Hasan *knew* that his *new* trousers were too long.

The words *new* and *knew* sound alike, but they have different spellings, and they have different meanings. *Knew* means "understood," and *new* means "never been used." Were you able to figure out the meanings of *new* and *knew* by the way the words were used in the sentence?

Sea and *see* is another example of a pair of words that sound the same but have different spellings and meanings. The word *sea* means "a body of water." *To see* is "what you do with your eyes."

The words *sea* and *see* sound right in the sentence below, but only one word has the right meaning. Which word belongs in the sentence?

Hasan is swimming in the ___.

How did you know which word to use? The fact that Hasan was swimming gave you a hint. Where might Hasan swim? He might swim in a *sea*.

Now read the following sentences. Tell which word from the pair of words makes sense in each sentence. Look for hints that will help you figure out which word belongs in each sentence.

1. The pants were not the ___ length.
   right   write
2. Nobody ___ shorten the trousers.
   wood   would
3. ___ Hasan shortened them himself.
   sew   so

What is special about the way Grandpa "sees"?

Through Grandpa's Eyes

by Patricia MacLachlan

Of all the houses that I know, I like my Grandpa's best. That's because I see it through Grandpa's eyes.

Grandpa is blind. He doesn't see the house the way I do. He has his own way of seeing.

In the morning, the sun pushes through the curtains into my eyes. I burrow down into the covers to get away, but the light follows me. I give up, throw back the covers, and run to Grandpa's room.

The sun wakes Grandpa differently from the way it wakes me. He says it touches him, *warming* him awake.

When I peek around the door, Grandpa is already up and doing his morning exercises. Bending and stretching by the bed, he stops and smiles because he hears me.

"Good morning, John."

"Where's Nana?" I ask him.

"Don't you know?" he says, bending and stretching. "Close your eyes, John, and look through my eyes."

I close my eyes. Down below, I hear the banging of pots and the sound of water running that I didn't hear before.

"Nana is in the kitchen, making breakfast," I say.

When I open my eyes again, I can see Grandpa nodding at me. He is tall with dark gray hair. And his eyes are sharp blue even if they are not sharp seeing.

"Breakfast!" calls Nana from downstairs.

"I smell eggs frying," says Grandpa. He bends his head close to mine. "And buttered toast."

The wooden banister on the stairway has been worn smooth from Grandpa running his fingers up and down. I walk behind him, my fingers following Grandpa's smooth path.

We go into the kitchen to eat our breakfast. When he eats, Grandpa's plate of food is a clock. "Two eggs at nine o'clock and toast at two o'clock," says Nana to Grandpa. "And a dollop of jam."

"A dollop of jam," I tell Grandpa, "at six o'clock."

I make my plate a clock, too, and eat through Grandpa's eyes.

Later, Grandpa and I walk outside, through the front yard, and across the field to the river. Grandpa has not been blind forever. He remembers in his mind the gleam of the sun on the river, the Queen Anne's lace in the meadow, and every rose in his garden. But he gently takes my elbow as we walk so that I can help show him the path.

"I feel a south wind," says Grandpa.

I can tell which way the wind is blowing because I see the way the tops of the trees lean. Grandpa tells by the feel of the meadow grasses and by the way his hair blows against his face.

I see a blackbird with a red patch on its wing sitting on a cattail. Without thinking, I point my finger. "What is that bird, Grandpa?" I ask excitedly.

"*Conk-a-ree,*" the bird calls to us.

"A red-winged blackbird," says Grandpa promptly. He can't see me pointing. But he hears the shrill song of the bird.

"And somewhere behind the blackbird," he says, listening, "a song sparrow."

I hear a scratchy song, and I look and look until I see the sand-colored bird that Grandpa knows is here.

As we walk back to the house, Grandpa stops suddenly. He bends his head to one side, listening. He points his finger upward.

"Honkers," he whispers.

I look up and see a flock of geese, high in the clouds, flying in a *V*.

"Canada geese," I tell him.

"Honkers," he insists. And we both laugh.

We walk up the path again and to the yard where Nana is painting the porch chairs. Grandpa smells the paint.

"What color, Nana?" he asks. "I cannot smell the color."

"Blue," I tell him, smiling. "Blue like the sky."

"Blue like the color of Grandpa's eyes," Nana says.

A long time ago, before I can remember, before Grandpa was blind, he did things the way I do. Now, when we drink tea and eat lunch on the porch, Grandpa fills his own cup of tea by putting his finger just inside the rim of the cup to tell him when it is full. He never burns his finger.

In the afternoon, Grandpa, Nana, and I take our books outside to read under the apple tree. Grandpa reads his book with his fingers, feeling the raised Braille dots that tell him the words.

As he reads, Grandpa laughs.

"Tell us what's funny," says Nana. "Read to us, Papa." And he does.

Nana and I put down our books to listen. A gray squirrel comes down the trunk of the apple tree, tail high, and seems to listen, too. But Grandpa doesn't see him.

After supper, Grandpa turns on the TV. I watch, but Grandpa listens, and the music and the words tell him when something is funny or sad.

Somehow, Grandpa knows when it is dark, and he takes me upstairs and tucks me into bed. He bends down to kiss me, his hands feeling my head.

"You need a haircut, John," he says.

Before Grandpa leaves, he pulls the light chain above my bed to turn out the light. But, by mistake, he's turned it on instead. I lie for a moment after he's gone, smiling, before I get up to turn off the light.

Then when it is dark for me the way it is dark for Grandpa, I hear the night noises that Grandpa hears—the house creaking, the birds singing their last songs of the day, the wind rustling the tree outside my window.

Then all of a sudden, I hear the sounds of geese overhead. They fly low over the house. "Grandpa," I call softly, hoping he hears them, too.

"Honkers," he calls back.

"Go to sleep, John," says Nana.

Grandpa says her voice smiles to him. I test it.

"What?" I call to her.

"I said go to sleep," she answers.

She says it sternly. But Grandpa is right. Her voice smiles to me. I know. Because I'm looking through Grandpa's eyes.

Discussing the Selection

1. What was special about the way Grandpa saw?
2. What were some ways that John saw "through Grandpa's eyes"?
3. Why did John smile after Grandpa tucked him in and left the room?
4. Find and read a part of the story where Grandpa could "see" something John couldn't.
5. Why do you think John wanted to see through his Grandpa's eyes?

Using Language

Making a Chart

Prewriting Grandpa was able to hear, feel, and smell things that helped him know what was happening around him. Copy the chart below onto a sheet of paper.

What Grandpa heard, smelled, or felt	What it told Grandpa

Writing Reread the story. As you read, find things that Grandpa heard, smelled, or felt. What did each thing tell Grandpa? Fill in the chart as you find things in the story.

Postwriting Copy the chart onto the chalkboard and take turns filling in the lines.

(To be read by the teacher)

Mimi's Fingers

I am blind. All that I can see
My enchanted fingers bring to me,
As if all sight were mingled with all touch
I do not mind not-seeing very much.
In Braille I read the words these fingers trace,
And with them come to know your smile, your face,
Your buckled shoes, the silk-thread of your hair,
The fabric of each suit and dress you wear;
All shapes, all sizes, how long, how far, how high,
How round a bowl, how gently curved the sky,
How pointed the far tip-top of a hill,
The narrow table of a window sill.
I know a snowflake as a melting star,
The sticky-thick of honey and of tar.
Color alone my fingers cannot do.
Could you, could you, tell me about blue?

Mary O'Neill

UNIT CLOSER

FAMILIES

The stories in this unit were about families. Tell how the members of each family treated one another. Think of some words you could use that would describe all the families. Then answer the following questions:

1. You read about some characters who learned something from their families. Who were these characters? What did they learn?

2. Tell why John liked to visit Grandpa's house in "Through Grandpa's Eyes." Then tell why Paco enjoyed his uncle's visits.

3. In what ways were Mona and Spray like people? How were they different?

4. What words could you use to describe both Grandma Tappleton, in "Thanksgiving at the Tappletons'," and Grandpa, in "Through Grandpa's Eyes"?

5. If you could visit a family from any story in this unit, which family would you visit? Why?

Bibliography

Books in This Unit

Nine True Dolphin Stories by Margaret Davidson. Hastings House, 1974.

Through Grandpa's Eyes by Patricia MacLachlan. Harper & Row, 1979.

Thanksgiving at the Tappletons' by Eileen Spinelli. Addison-Wesley, 1982.

New Patches for Old by Barbara K. Walker. Parents' Magazine Press, 1974.

To Hilda for Helping by Margot Zemach. Farrar, Straus & Giroux, 1977.

Additional Books to Read

Aunt Nina and Her Nephews and Nieces by Franz Brandenberg. Greenwillow, 1983.

A Three Hat Day by Laura Geringer. Harper & Row, 1985.

The Relatives Came by Cynthia Rylant. Bradbury Press, 1985.

UNIT 2

SOMETHING'S MISSING

"Where did I put that book?" "How could I lose a mitten?" "Why did my best friend move away?" "Who took my pencil?" These are the kinds of questions you might ask yourself when you discover that something's missing. It may be as small as a mitten or as important as a friend.

Each of the stories in this unit is about something that is missing. In the first story, you'll read about a boy who misses a friend who has just moved away. Next you'll read a two-part story about a detective who tracks down missing dogs. Then you'll learn how the author of the detective story became a writer. In another story, you'll read what happens when a farmer discovers something missing from his garden. Finally, you'll see what two friends decide to do because they think something is missing in their lives.

As you read this unit, think about these questions: What is missing in each story? How is each character's life affected by what's missing?

Jimmy misses his best friend, William, who has just moved away. Will he find another special friend?

My Friend William Moved Away

by Martha Whitmore Hickman

My friend William moved away yesterday. He lived on my street—three houses down—by the fruit tree and the fire plug and the crack in the sidewalk with grass in it. We played together almost every day, at my house or at William's.

Yesterday, the moving crew was at William's house all day. William and I watched them. Mary Ellen watched, too. She lives down the street and is in William's and my room at school.

When the movers left, William's father called, "Come on, William. We have to get going."

We all went to the car. I stood on the sidewalk with my mother and father and waved. "So long, William," I said.

This morning when I woke up, I remembered about William and felt sad. After a while, I got up and put on my favorite shirt and blue jeans. I drank some juice and ate breakfast. I talked to my hamsters. I watched TV.

This afternoon, I went to William's old house. It was there all right, but no William. I started to go back home.

When I was almost home, I had an idea. I turned around and walked past William's house to Mary Ellen's house. I went up the porch steps and waited to see if Mary Ellen might come out. She didn't, so I rang the doorbell. Nobody came, so I started to scoot off the porch. Then someone opened the door and said, "Jimmy!" It was Mary Ellen.

"Hello," I said. "Can you come out?"

"I'll ask my mother," she said.

While Mary Ellen was away, I looked at her bike on the porch. It has a rocket on the side and blue streamers.

"You can ride it," Mary Ellen said when she came back.

"Thanks," I said. "You want to bring it up to my house, and I'll get mine?"

"Sure," she said.

We walked to my house, past William's house, and Mary Ellen pushed her bike along beside us.

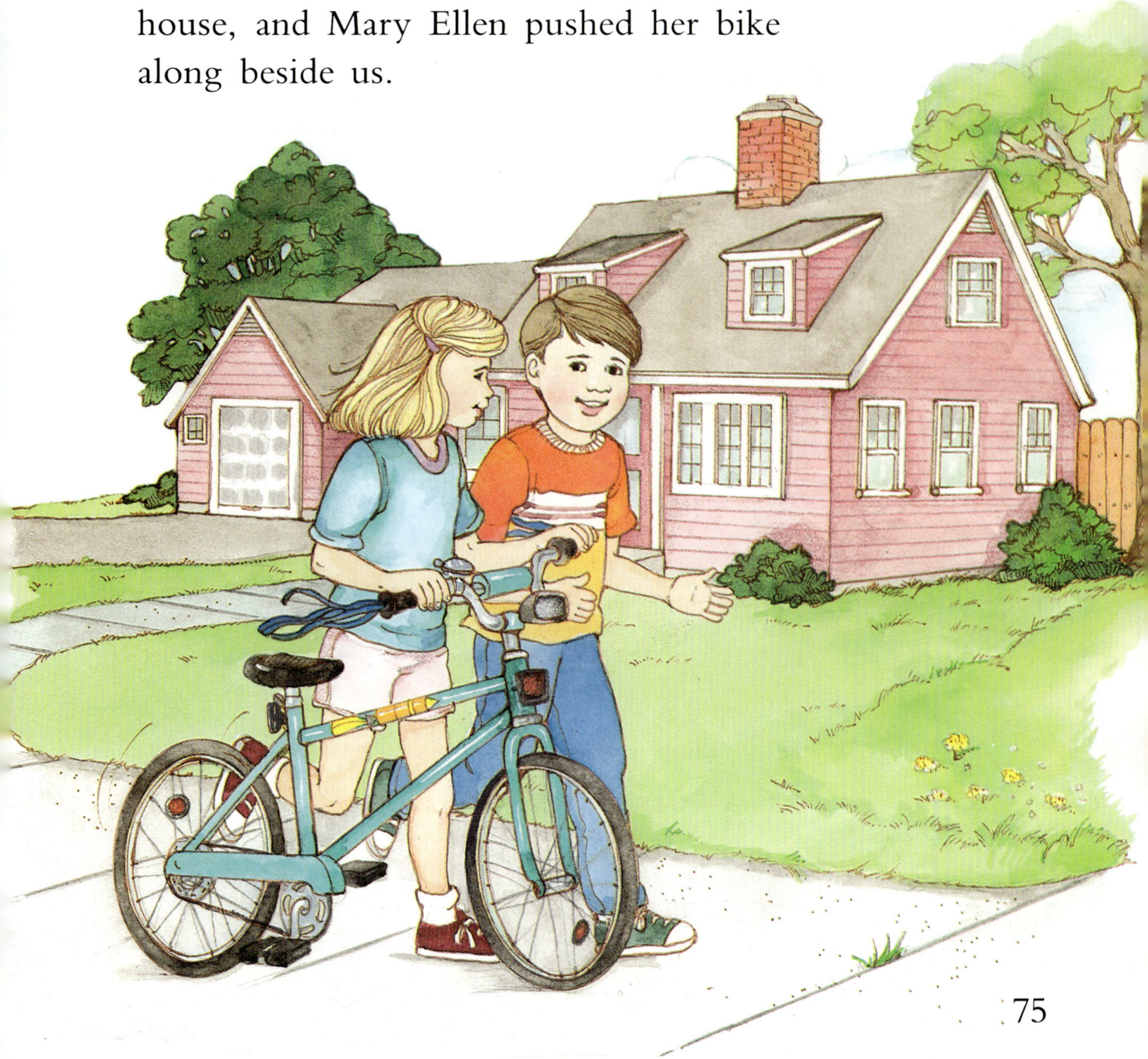

"You want to come in first?" I asked when we got to my house.

We went inside, and I showed her my hamsters. She put her finger out for one to chew on. "I have gerbils," she said. "Sometime you may come to see them."

We went outside and rode our bikes. We rode past William's house and past Mary Ellen's and past two boys playing.

We came back to my house and sat on the steps. After a while, I told Mary Ellen how funny it was not having William around.

"I know," she said. "I saw you and William walking to school together."

"Where were you?" I said.

"Sometimes I was walking way behind you," she said, "by myself."

"Oh," I said, thinking about it.

While we sat there, a bluejay flew into a tree. Then a truck went past, and some big boys on bikes.

The telephone rang inside. My mother called, "Mary Ellen, your mother wants you home for supper."

"Do you want to come over tomorrow?" Mary Ellen asked as she stood up.

"Sure," I said.

She got on her bike and rode away. At William's house, she waved back to me, and I waved, too.

I ran inside to talk to my hamsters. "Ralph," I said, "Henry"—those are my hamsters—"that was Mary Ellen. I'm going to her house tomorrow."

The hamsters just ran around on their wheel. *Squeak, squeak*, the wheel said, around and around, singing a song of a new friend and a nice day after all.

Discussing the Selection

1. Did Jimmy find another special friend? Explain your answer.
2. Why did Jimmy have trouble getting out of bed the day after William moved?
3. Why did Jimmy go to Mary Ellen's house?
4. Find and read the part of the story where Jimmy learned that Mary Ellen had lonely times, too.
5. If you were Jimmy, what would you have done the day after William moved?

Using Language

Writing Letters

Prewriting In "My Friend William Moved Away," you read that Jimmy felt sad when William moved. Think how William may have felt when he moved to a new place.

Writing Work with a friend. One of you pretend to be William. The other can be Jimmy. Write a letter to each other. Have William tell Jimmy about his new house and new friends. Have Jimmy tell how he feels because William is gone and what he and the rest of his friends have been doing.

Postwriting Have Jimmy and William read their letters to one another. Then share the letters with the rest of the class.

(To be read by the teacher)

I Loved My Friend

I loved my friend.
He went away from me.
There's nothing more to say.
The poem ends,
Soft as it began—
I loved my friend.

Langston Hughes

People pay Jane Martin to find lost dogs. What clues might help her find Barney, a missing dog?

Jane Martin, Dog Detective

Part 1

by Eve Bunting

A girl came to Jane Martin's tree house, and Jane could see that she was sad.

"I hope you are a good dog detective," the girl said. "I need you to find my dog. He has been lost for two weeks."

"Two weeks!" Jane said. "That is a long time. Did you look in the animal shelter?"

"He is not there."

Jane opened her notebook. "I need to know your name and the dog's name."

"I am Kay Newton, and my dog is Barney. Here's a picture I drew of him."

"The picture will help," Jane said. Barney was a black poodle. He had a red collar. "What can you tell me about Barney?"

"Every day, Barney went out by himself," said Kay. "But he always came home. Two weeks ago, he went out and did not come back."

"It is not good to let dogs run free," Jane said.

Kay's face got red. "I know, but he liked to go."

"Tell me some more about Barney," Jane said.

Kay thought. "He can beg and give his paw." She thought some more. "He loves ice cream and running after trucks."

Jane smiled and said, "He is a real dog!"

Jane wrote everything in her notebook. "Come to my tree house tomorrow," she told Kay. "Perhaps I will have some news about Barney."

"I hope it will not cost too much," Kay said. "I only have five dollars."

"My fee is twenty-five cents a day," Jane said. "Have no fear. I work quickly."

Kay took twenty-five cents from her pocket.

"I will go to work right away," Jane said. They shook hands.

First, Jane checked with all the kids on her street. She showed them the picture of Barney. "Have you seen this dog?" she asked. It was hard work—the kind of work detectives must do.

Most of the kids knew Barney. "He runs down this street every day," one boy said. "He goes around that corner, but I have not seen him for a long time."

"Thank you." Jane went around the corner.

A woman was working in her yard. Jane showed her dog-detective card, and then she showed Barney's picture.

"Barney passes here all the time," the woman said. "I think he goes into the park, but I have not seen him for a week or two."

"Thank you," Jane said.

Jane went to the park and walked on all the paths. She was looking for clues. There was a bit of ice-cream cone on the grass. Jane picked it up. "No," she said, "this was not Barney's cone. Barney would have eaten all of it."

The cone gave her an idea.

There was a shop near the entrance to the park. Jane got a dish of ice cream. It cost twenty-five cents, but to a good detective, money is not everything. Jane put the ice cream beside a light pole. Dogs like light poles, and dogs are good smellers. Barney loved ice cream. He might smell this and come for it.

Flies came, and ants came. A white cat came. A bluejay came and chased the cat. A black dog came, but it was not Barney.

Jane shooed them all away. The ice cream melted. A chipmunk came, and Jane let it have the ice cream. Then she threw the dish in the trash and went home.

Kay came the next day.

"No luck," Jane told her, "but I have a new idea. Barney went out every day. Did he always go at the same time?"

Kay nodded. "At three. He came back at four."

"Hm," said Jane, tapping her head. That helped her think. "What happens at three every day?" she asked herself.

She answered herself: "Kids get out of school, but this is summer. There is no school, but the time is a clue." She tapped her head again. "Come back tomorrow, Kay, and I may have Barney."

"Here is your fee for today," Kay said.

Jane took the twenty-five cents. "Thank you," she said. "I gave a party with the last twenty-five cents."

"A party?"

"Never mind," Jane said. Good detectives keep secrets.

Discussing the Selection

1. What clues has Jane Martin found so far that might lead her to Barney?
2. Why did Kay Newton let her dog go out by himself?
3. Why did Jane buy the dish of ice cream?
4. Find and read a part of the story that tells how Jane acted like a real detective.
5. What do you think Jane meant when she said she "gave a party with the last twenty-five cents"?

Using Language

Being a Word Detective

Prewriting In the story, Jane Martin was a dog detective. See if you can be a word detective. In the sentences below, the words have no spaces between them.

Barneyisablackpoodle.
Hehasaredcollar.
Hecanbeg.
Helovesicecream.
Herunsaftertrucks.

Writing Decide what each sentence says. Then write the sentences, leaving space between each word. Get together with a friend and read the sentences. Then write some sentences of your own, without leaving spaces between the words.

Postwriting Take turns trying to read the sentences that each of you has written.

Jane Martin is still looking for Barney. Read to see if she solves the case.

Jane Martin, Dog Detective

Part 2

by Eve Bunting

The next day at three o'clock, Jane started from Barney's house. She walked as fast as a poodle would run. She walked along the street, around the corner, past the woman's yard, into the park.

This was an old detective trick she had learned. It was called "tracing the steps of the lost dog."

Jane kept walking. This time she was looking for a *why*. *Why* did Barney come here each day at three? She hoped she would know the *why* when she saw it.

Then she *heard* it—a tune—a happy tune! And then she saw it! The *why* was an ice-cream truck. Of course! Barney had come to meet this truck each day.

The truck moved slowly, and the happy tune played over and over.

Jane ran toward it and held up her hand. A man put his head out of the window. He was smiling. "What would you like?"

Jane showed the man the picture. "Have you seen—" she started to ask. Then she stopped. A black poodle was on the seat beside the man. Its collar was blue, not red.

"Barney?" Jane said.

"Wuff!" The little dog wagged his tail.

The man was not smiling now. "This dog's name is not Barney. This dog is Fang, and he is my dog."

"How long have you had him?" Jane asked.

"A while."

"Two weeks?" Jane asked.

"About that. He was a stray. He was living in the park, and each day he ran after my truck."

"Aha," Jane said.

"I gave him ice cream."

"Aha again," Jane said.

"He was no one's dog," the man said to her, "so I took him, and now he rides with me. It's nice for both of us."

"This is Kay Newton's dog. She has been worried about him." Jane showed the man her dog detective card. "I must take him. I have been working on the case for the past two days."

The man petted Barney. "That girl must not like her dog," he said. "She let him run free. Dogs should not be in the park alone. I keep Fang on a long leash so he cannot jump out and get hurt."

"Barney cannot jump out and run home," Jane said. "He would if he could."

"He would not. He loves me." The man looked sad.

Jane was sorry for him. "Why don't you get your own dog? You could go to the animal shelter. There are good dogs there. Any dog would like to ride with you, but this is Kay Newton's dog."

The man petted Barney. "He wants to stay with me."

"Take off the leash," Jane said, "and we will see."

The man took a dish of ice cream from the freezer and pulled off the lid. He put the dish on the seat beside Barney.

"Here, Fang," he said. "Stay, Fang." He took the leash from the door handle. "Stay, Fang."

Barney cocked his head and looked at the ice cream. He looked at the man. He looked at the open window. "Wuff!" he said. He jumped and was gone. His leash trailed behind him.

"I did not think that dog would say no to ice cream," the man said. "That dog must really love Kay Newton."

"You took off his collar, didn't you?" Jane asked.

"I did not. He didn't have a collar. Kids in the park probably took it off. They take the collars off a lot of dogs."

"I see," said Jane.

"I did not try to find Barney's owner," the man said. "That was bad, but I wanted him very much."

"All is well that ends well," Jane said to the man. "Now all you have to do is go pick out a dog of your own at the animal shelter."

The man gave her a dish of ice cream. Jane ate it as she walked. It was good ice cream. She could see why Barney chased this truck. Then Jane sat on a bench and wrote in her notebook:

The ice-cream man did it.
Barney Case closed.
Signed, Jane Martin, Dog Detective.

Discussing the Selection

1. How did Jane Martin solve the case?
2. Why did the ice-cream man decide to keep Barney?
3. What happened when Jane asked the ice-cream man if he had seen Barney?
4. Find and read the part of the story where the ice-cream man knew he was wrong for keeping Barney.
5. Do you think Jane Martin was a good detective? Why or why not?

Using Language

Putting Things in Order

Prewriting When you read, it is important to remember the order in which things happen. Think about the order in the story you have just read.

Writing The sentences below tell what Jane did in the story, but they are not in the right order. Write the sentences in the order in which they happened.

Jane saw a poodle on the seat.
Jane ran toward the truck.
Jane showed the picture of Barney to the ice-cream man.
Jane saw an ice-cream truck.

Postwriting Compare your list of sentences to a friend's list. If your sentences are in a different order, reread the story to find the correct order.

Searching for a way to keep busy led Eve Bunting to write books for children. Why does she enjoy being a writer?

Meet Eve Bunting

by Carol Peske

"The thing I like most about writing is being a storyteller," says Eve Bunting. She is the author of the book *Jane Martin, Dog Detective.*

Ms. Bunting was born in Ireland and lived there for the first thirty years of her life. In 1959, she came to the United States with her husband and three young children.

Ms. Bunting became a writer almost by accident. When her children got older, she was searching for a way to keep busy. She heard about a writing class at a college near her home and decided to take it.

In the class, Ms. Bunting met a lot of people who were interested in writing. The class was run like a workshop. Each member would share his or her work with the rest of the class, and then the class would talk about it. Ms. Bunting worked hard and listened to what her classmates said about her writing.

Her first book, *Two Giants*, was published in 1972. Since then, Ms. Bunting has written over one hundred books for children of many different ages.

Where does she get the ideas for so many books? Ms. Bunting says an idea for a book can come from almost anywhere.

For example, one day she was reading a newspaper article about a man who was a dog detective. People would pay him to find their lost dogs. He was very good at what he did.

Ms. Bunting thought a story about a dog detective would be a great idea for a children's book. She decided to make her dog detective a young girl named Jane Martin.

Ms. Bunting had Jane Martin do many of the same things the real-life dog detective did. The real-life dog detective put up signs so people would know about him, and so did Jane Martin. He charged a fee to find people's dogs, and so did Jane Martin. He was a hard worker, and so was Jane Martin. He had his own office, and so did Jane Martin, even if her office was in a tree house.

Today, Ms. Bunting still finds writing very worthwhile. She especially likes to hear from the children who read and enjoy her books.

Each story she writes is a new adventure for her. "Writing is like living in a fantasy world," says the author. "You can make up stories about anything you want."

Discussing the Selection

1. How did Eve Bunting become a writer?
2. Where does she get ideas for her books?
3. Why did she decide to take a writing class?
4. How did Eve Bunting make Jane Martin like a real detective?

Using Language

Being an Author

Prewriting Eve Bunting has written over one hundred books. Read the part of the selection again that explained how she gets ideas for stories. Then make a list of ideas for some stories that you would like to write.

Writing Choose one story idea and make a list of all the things that will happen in the story. Then write the story.

Postwriting Share your story with three friends. Save the list that you made for the next time you need an idea for a story.

(To be read by the teacher)

Hideout

They looked for me
and from my nook
inside the oak
I watched them look.

Through little slits
between the leaves
I saw their looking
legs and sleeves.

They would have looked
all over town
except—
I threw some acorns down.

Aileen Fisher

COMPREHENSION/
THINKING SKILL

You Be the Detective

As Jane Martin searched for Barney, she collected the following clues:

1. Barney loved ice cream.
2. Barney went out by himself every day at three o'clock.
3. Barney passed the same house every day and went into the park.
4. Jane saw the ice-cream truck in the park at three o'clock.
5. The ice-cream man had a dog in his truck.

Using these clues, Jane solved the case. No one told Jane what happened to Barney. She looked at the clues and filled in the rest of the information herself. The reader could have solved the case using the same clues. Did you know what had happened to Barney when Jane did?

Read the following story. Look for clues to solve the mystery.

> Mrs. Knox had just fixed lunch for herself when the telephone rang. She set her lunch on the table and went to answer it. She came back to find her sandwich gone, the plate on the floor, and mud on the table.
>
> Who ate her sandwich—her six-year-old son, John, or the dog? Mrs. Knox was pretty sure it was the dog. Then John came in and said, "I'm starved." Now Mrs. Knox was sure the dog had eaten her lunch.

At first, Mrs. Knox wasn't sure who had eaten her sandwich. She knew that both a dog and a six-year-old could push a plate to the floor. What made her sure the dog had eaten her sandwich? If John had just eaten a sandwich, he wouldn't have been "starved."

When you know how to put the clues together, solving mysteries can be fun.

Some lettuce is missing from a farmer's garden. Read to see what makes the thief so clever.

Mr. Rabbit and Mr. Bear

by Julius Lester

If there was one thing in the world Mr. Rabbit liked, it was lettuce. He would do anything to get lettuce.

Well, one day Mr. Rabbit was hopping down the road when he saw that he was passing a field of lettuce. He had never seen so much lettuce in all his life. As far as he could see, there were rows and rows and rows and rows and rows of lettuce. The only thing that stood between him and all those rows and rows and rows and rows of lettuce was a wire fence.

"What am I going to do?" asked Mr. Rabbit as he hopped alongside the fence. "I have to have some of that lettuce."

Anyone else would have given up, but not Mr. Rabbit. He went across the road and sat down under a big oak tree to think. He hadn't been sitting there long when a little girl walked across the road, unlocked the gate to the field of lettuce, and went inside.

"That's it!" Mr. Rabbit shouted, leaping up. "Tomorrow I'll come back at the same time, and if the little girl comes again, I'll get her to let me in."

The next day, Mr. Rabbit was sitting by the gate, waiting for the little girl. After a while, she came out of the woods.

"Good morning, little girl," said Mr. Rabbit. "The farmer said that you should let me into the field."

"Oh, certainly, Mr. Rabbit," the little girl said. She unlocked the gate, and Mr. Rabbit hopped through.

"Thank you," said Mr. Rabbit. "Now you be sure to come and reopen the gate at noon."

"All right, Mr. Rabbit."

Mr. Rabbit hopped to a far corner of the field and began eating. He had never tasted such crispy, yummy lettuce in *aaaaaaall* of his life. And he ate and ate and ate, and then ate some more. When noon came, he was ready to go. He'd eaten so much, it was all he could do to hop to the fence and have the little girl let him out.

Every morning, Mr. Rabbit came back, and every morning, the little girl would let him in.

After several weeks, the farmer started noticing that a lot of his lettuce was missing. He decided to hide behind a tree and see if he could learn who had been eating his lettuce.

The next morning, the farmer was there bright and early, and he saw Mr. Rabbit hop up to the gate. Then he saw his little girl come out of the woods, cross the road, and unlock the gate to let Mr. Rabbit into the field of crispy, yummy lettuce. The farmer was angry, but not at his little girl. He knew Mr. Rabbit had tricked her, and he was sure angry at the rabbit.

Mr. Rabbit didn't know that his lettuce-eating days were almost over. He was too busy enjoying that lettuce. Chomp! Chomp! Chomp! He was eating so fast that he didn't hear the farmer sneak into the field. The next thing Mr. Rabbit knew, someone had him by the scruff of his neck, yelling, "I've got you now, Mr. Rabbit! I'm going to teach you a lesson."

The farmer took Mr. Rabbit out to a big tree. There he tied one end of a rope around Mr. Rabbit's leg and tied the other end of the rope to a limb of the tree. And there was poor Mr. Rabbit, hanging in the air by one leg, swinging back and forth.

"I'm going to leave you there for a while, Mr. Rabbit, to teach you a lesson."

The farmer went away, leaving Mr. Rabbit swinging back and forth, back and forth. Anybody else would've been scared hanging up there in the middle of the air by one leg, but Mr. Rabbit was already busy thinking about how he was going to get down.

He was thinking and thinking and thinking, swinging back and forth, back and forth. He was thinking so hard that he didn't notice Mr. Bear looking up at him.

"What are you doing up there, Mr. Rabbit?" asked Mr. Bear.

"I'm resting," Mr. Rabbit said.

Mr. Bear scratched his head. "Looks to me like you're tied to that limb by one leg."

"That's right, Mr. Bear. That's the new way of resting. It's much better than lying in a bed."

"Would you mind if I tried it, Mr. Rabbit?" asked Mr. Bear.

Mr. Rabbit thought for a minute. "Well, I don't know, Mr. Bear."

"Aw, please, Mr. Rabbit?"

"Well, all right, but don't rest too long, Mr. Bear. I know you. You'll get up here and enjoy it so much that I'll never get to rest again."

"I promise, Mr. Rabbit."

"OK. Untie this rope."

Mr. Bear reached up and untied the rope from Mr. Rabbit's leg. Then Mr. Rabbit helped Mr. Bear put the rope around his leg and retie it. "Doesn't that feel good, Mr. Bear?"

Mr. Bear was swinging back and forth, upside down, but he nodded. "It sure does, Mr. Rabbit."

"Well, I'm going down to the creek to get me a drink of water, Mr. Bear. I'll be back in a little while."

"OK, Mr. Rabbit."

But Mr. Bear never saw Mr. Rabbit again that day.

When the farmer came back to see if Mr. Rabbit had learned his lesson, he was surprised and angry to see Mr. Bear hanging up there instead. But Mr. Rabbit was long gone by that time. All the farmer could do was let Mr. Bear down and hope that he would get Mr. Rabbit another time.

Discussing the Selection

1. How did you know Mr. Rabbit was very clever?
2. What trick did Mr. Rabbit use to get into the lettuce field?
3. How did the farmer catch Mr. Rabbit?
4. Reread the part where you first knew that Mr. Rabbit had tricked Mr. Bear.
5. How do you think Mr. Bear felt when Mr. Rabbit didn't come back?

Using Language

Putting on a Puppet Show

Planning Get together with three friends to put on a puppet show of "Mr. Rabbit and Mr. Bear." Decide who will be Mr. Rabbit, the little girl, the farmer, and Mr. Bear.

Working Together Make puppets from four paper bags. Make each paper bag look like a story character. You might use colored paper, markers, yarn, and anything else you'd like to make your puppets. Then practice acting out "Mr. Rabbit and Mr. Bear," using the puppets.

Sharing Put on the puppet show for other groups in your class.

DECODING/
VOCABULARY SKILL

Making New Words

Read the following sentence about the farmer's daughter from the story "Mr. Rabbit and Mr. Bear."

> She unlocked the gate, and Mr.
> Rabbit hopped through.

In this sentence, what does the word *unlocked* mean? *Unlocked* means the gate was not locked. *Un-* was added to the word *locked* to make a new word with a new meaning. *Unlocked* means "not locked." *Un-* at the beginning of a word means "not."

A **prefix** is a word part you add to the beginning of a word to make a new word. Adding a prefix to a word changes the meaning of the word. *Un-* is a prefix that means "not."

What do the following words mean?

unhappy unlike unreal

Read the following sentence from the story where Mr. Rabbit was talking to the farmer's daughter.

"Now be sure to come and reopen the gate at noon."

In this sentence, what does the word *reopen* mean? *Reopen* means "to open again." The prefix *re-* was added to the word *open* to make a new word with a new meaning. The prefix *re-* means "again."

Read the following words and tell what they mean.

redo refill rerun

When you read a word that has the prefix *un-* or *re-,* try to figure out the meaning of the word. Remember that the prefix *un-* means "not," and the prefix *re-* means "again."

Two friends think that changing places will help them find what's missing from their lives. What will they learn?

Gabrielle and Selena

by Peter Desbarats

Gabrielle and Selena went everywhere and did everything together. They were like sisters.

One summer day, they were sitting under Mr. Simon's lilac tree, part-way between Gabrielle's house and Selena's house. Gabrielle said, "Sometimes I wish, Selena, that I were you."

"Why do you want to be me?" asked Selena.

Gabrielle put her chin on her hands and said, "I'm tired of being myself. Every morning I wake up in the same room, say hello to the same father and mother, and eat the same breakfast. I think it would be more interesting to live at your house."

"But it's the same at my house," said Selena. "I do almost the same things that you do every day."

"But you don't do them *exactly* the same," said Gabrielle. "I think it would be more fun if I could be you and you could be me."

"That's silly," said Selena.

"No, it isn't," said Gabrielle. "All we have to do is put our hands and feet together, like this, and I'll look into your eyes, like this, and . . ."

Selena started to laugh and said, "Your eyes look funny."

"Stop fooling around, or it won't work," said Gabrielle. "Now we turn around once, and I say—'I am Selena.' "

"And I say—'I am Gabrielle,' " said Selena.

The girls took two steps backward and looked at each other.

"Hi, Gabrielle," said Gabrielle.

"Hi, Selena," said Selena.

"Well," said Gabrielle, "it's almost time for supper, so I'd better hurry. Good-by, Gabrielle. Have fun at my house. I mean, *your* house."

"Good-by, Selena," said Selena, "and don't forget to feed my cat. I mean, *your* cat."

When Gabrielle reached Selena's house, she rang the doorbell. Selena's mother opened the door and said, "Hello, Gabrielle."

"I'm not Gabrielle," said Gabrielle. "I'm Selena."

"Oh, I see," said Selena's mother. "Well, Selena, I don't understand why you rang the doorbell. Selena always just walks into the house."

"I forgot," said Gabrielle, and she walked into the house.

"It's almost time for supper," said Selena's mother. "We're having your favorite vegetable—turnips."

"Turnips are my favorite vegetable?" asked Gabrielle, who couldn't stand them.

"Certainly they are," said Selena's mother. "You always have two helpings."

"Yuck!" said Gabrielle to herself.

When Selena reached Gabrielle's house, she walked right in. She went into the kitchen where Gabrielle's mother was and said, "What's for supper?"

"Oh," said Gabrielle's mother, "are you staying for supper, Selena?"

"Of course I am," said Selena, "and my name's Gabrielle."

Gabrielle's mother turned around and looked at her. "Where's Gabrielle? I mean, where's Selena?" she asked.

"Selena's at my house," said Selena. "I mean, *her* house."

"Very well, Gabrielle," said Gabrielle's mother. "Wash your hands for supper. We're having your favorite—a great big omelet."

"That's my favorite?" asked Selena.

"I always give you an extra-big helping," said Gabrielle's mother.

"Yuck!" said Selena to herself.

Later, when Gabrielle had finished most of her turnips, Selena's father said, "Now it's time to wash the dishes."

"Wash the dishes?" said Gabrielle in a small voice filled with sadness. "But I always watch TV after supper."

"You never watch TV, Selena," said Selena's mother. "You always say it's much more fun to wash the dishes."

At Gabrielle's house, Selena was sweeping the floor. Gabrielle's mother had said that this was what Gabrielle did every night before she went to bed at seven-thirty.

"Do you mean *I* have to go to bed at seven-thirty?" asked Selena.

"Good heavens, you don't *have* to. You *want* to," said Gabrielle's mother. "Every time I ask you to watch TV with me, you say it's much better to go to bed early."

"Well!" said Selena to herself. "No wonder Gabrielle wanted to be me. This is a terrible way to live."

At Selena's house, Gabrielle had just finished the dishes when Selena's father said, "Time for bed, Selena."

"But it's only seven-thirty," said Gabrielle.

"Is it that late?" said Selena's father. "My goodness, by this time you're usually sound asleep on the back porch."

"The *back porch*?" said Gabrielle.

"You always say it's healthy to sleep outside," said Selena's father.

"Boy!" said Gabrielle to herself. "I never realized Selena was such a nut."

Gabrielle looked up at Selena's father and said, "I'm going home."

"All right," said Selena's father, smiling. "Good night, Gabrielle."

Gabrielle and Selena met on the sidewalk under the streetlight by Mr. Simon's lilac tree.

"Hello, Selena," said Selena, looking at Gabrielle.

"Never mind calling me Selena," said Gabrielle. "I wouldn't be you for all the money in the world. You didn't tell me turnips were your favorite vegetable."

"*Turnips*?" said Selena. "I can't stand turnips. You didn't tell me you loved omelets."

"Yuck!" said Gabrielle. "I hate omelets almost as much as I hate washing dishes."

"But you sweep the kitchen floor every night," said Selena.

"I do not," said Gabrielle, "and at least I don't sleep on the back porch."

"Who sleeps on the back porch?" cried Selena.

"But your father said . . ." said Gabrielle.

"And your mother said . . ." said Selena.

Suddenly, the two girls looked at each other and started to laugh. And their laughter sounded like silver bells beneath the streetlights beneath the stars beneath the soft black sky.

Discussing the Selection

1. What did Gabrielle and Selena learn by changing places?
2. Why did Gabrielle and Selena decide to change places?
3. What happened when Gabrielle and Selena each arrived at the other's house?
4. Find and read the part of the story where each girl decided to be herself.
5. Why did Gabrielle's and Selena's parents say their daughters did things they really didn't do?

Using Language

Making Up a Conversation

Planning At the end of the story, Gabrielle and Selena talked to each other about what had happened when they changed places. The story ended when Gabrielle and Selena finally understood that their parents had played a trick on them.

Working Together Get together with a friend. One of you pretend to be Gabrielle and the other pretend to be Selena. Find the part near the end of the story where they met each under under the lilac tree. Read the lines that they said to each other. Make up some more things that the girls might have said if the story had not ended there.

Sharing Share your conversation with the rest of the class.

UNIT CLOSER

SOMETHING'S MISSING

The stories you read in this unit were each about something that was missing.

Think about what was missing in each story and why it was missing. How was each character's life affected by what was missing? Then answer the following questions:

1. Think how Jimmy felt when William moved away. What characters in "Jane Martin, Dog Detective" might have felt the same way? Why?
2. Gabrielle and Selena wanted to trade places. In what other story did two characters trade places? Why?
3. List some words that might describe a good detective. Then tell what characters in this unit acted like detectives.
4. Think how the main characters felt throughout each story. Which characters felt differently at the end of the story than they did at the beginning? Why?

Bibliography

Books in This Unit

Jane Martin, Dog Detective by Eve Bunting. Harcourt Brace Jovanovich, 1984.

Gabrielle and Selena by Peter Desbarats. Harcourt, Brace & World, 1968.

My Friend William Moved Away by Martha Whitmore Hickman. Abbingdon Press, 1979.

The Knee-High Man and Other Tales by Julius Lester. Dial, 1972.

Additional Books to Read

The Traveling Men of Ballycoo by Eve Bunting. Harcourt Brace Jovanovich, 1983.

The Foundling by Carol Carrick. Clarion, 1977.

Jamaica's Find by Juanita Havill. Houghton Mifflin, 1986.

UNIT 3

A DIFFERENT WAY

There are many different ways to do everyday things. People wear different kinds of clothes. They eat different kinds of food, and they speak different languages.

The first story in this unit is about a young goat who eats differently from the way most goats eat. In the next story, you'll read about two baseball players who play the game in a most unusual way. Then you'll find out what makes the octopus so different from other animals. You'll read about a little girl who must find a different way to get a birthday present for her grandfather. Finally, you'll see how a woman deals with a giant, who comes to visit her husband, in a way different than you might expect.

As you read each of the stories, think about the following questions: Which characters behave in a way that is different from what you expected? What makes their behavior different?

A young goat eats differently than his parents think he should. Will he learn to eat the way most goats do?

Gregory, the Terrible Eater

by Mitchell Sharmat

Once there was a goat named Gregory. Gregory liked to jump from rock to rock, kick his legs into the air, and butt his head against walls.

"I'm an average goat," said Gregory.

But Gregory was not an average goat. Gregory was a terrible eater. Every time he sat down to eat with his mother and father, he knew he was in for trouble.

"Would you like a tin can, Gregory?" asked Mother Goat.

"No, thanks," said Gregory.

"How about a nice box, a piece of rug, and a bottle cap?" asked Father Goat.

"Baaaaaa," said Gregory sadly.

"Well, I think this is a meal fit for a goat," said Mother Goat as she chewed on an old shoe.

"It certainly is," said Father Goat as he ate a shirt. "I don't know why you're such a fussy eater, Gregory."

"I'm not fussy," said Gregory. "I just want fruits, vegetables, eggs, fish, bread, and butter—good stuff like that."

Mother Goat stopped eating the shoe. "Now what kind of food is *that*, Gregory?" she said.

"It's what I like," said Gregory.

"It's terrible," said Father Goat. He wiped his mouth with his napkin.

After Gregory was excused from the table, Mother and Father Goat ate their evening newspaper in silence.

The next morning Father Goat said, "Gregory just isn't eating right. We must take him to see Dr. Ram."

So off they went to see Dr. Ram.

"What seems to be the trouble?" Dr. Ram asked.

"Gregory is a terrible eater," said Mother Goat. "We've offered him the best—shoes, boxes, cans. But all he wants are fruits and other horrible things."

"What do you have to say about all of this, Gregory?" asked Dr. Ram.

"I want what I like," said Gregory.

"Makes sense," said Dr. Ram. He turned to Mother and Father Goat. "I've treated picky eaters before. A taste for good food comes slowly. Try giving Gregory one new food each day until he eats everything."

And that's what they did.

One evening two weeks later, Father Goat asked, "Has anyone seen my striped necktie?"

"Not since breakfast," said Mother Goat. "Come to think of it, I haven't seen my sewing basket today."

"I think Gregory is eating too much," Father Goat said.

"Yes," said Mother Goat. "We'll have to do something about it."

The next evening Mother and Father Goat went to the dump. They came home with ten flat tires, a broken violin, and an old garden hose. They piled everything in front of Gregory's sandbox.

When Gregory came home for supper, he said, "What's all that stuff in the yard?"

"Your supper," said Father Goat.

"It all looks good," said Gregory.

Gregory ate the tires and the violin. But when he started in on the garden hose, he said, "I think I'm getting sick."

Gregory went to his room to lie down.

"I think Gregory ate too much junk," said Father Goat.

"Let's hope so," said Mother Goat.

All night, Gregory tossed and twisted.

The next morning he went down for breakfast. "What would you like for breakfast, Gregory?" asked Father Goat.

"Scrambled eggs, two pieces of waxed paper, and some juice," said Gregory.

"That sounds just about right," said Mother Goat. And it was.

Discussing the Selection

1. How did Gregory learn to eat the way most goats eat?
2. Why was Gregory a terrible eater for a goat?
3. What happened when Gregory's parents came home with things from the dump?
4. Reread the part of the story where Gregory started eating like a goat.
5. What do you think the story is saying about the way people should eat?

Making a Picture Chart

Planning In the story, Gregory's parents wanted him to eat things that other goats eat. What are some things you eat because they are good for you?

Working Together Find and cut out pictures of foods that are good for people to eat. Then cut out pictures that show some things that goats might like to eat. On a sheet of paper, write the headings below. Then paste each picture under the correct heading.

What People Eat	What Goats Eat

Discuss how the groups are alike and how they are different.

Sharing Put the charts from your class into a book. Did others in your class find the same kinds of pictures that you did?

STUDY SKILL

Reading a Bar Graph

What kinds of food do Gregory and his classmates like to eat for lunch? You can find out by looking at the chart below.

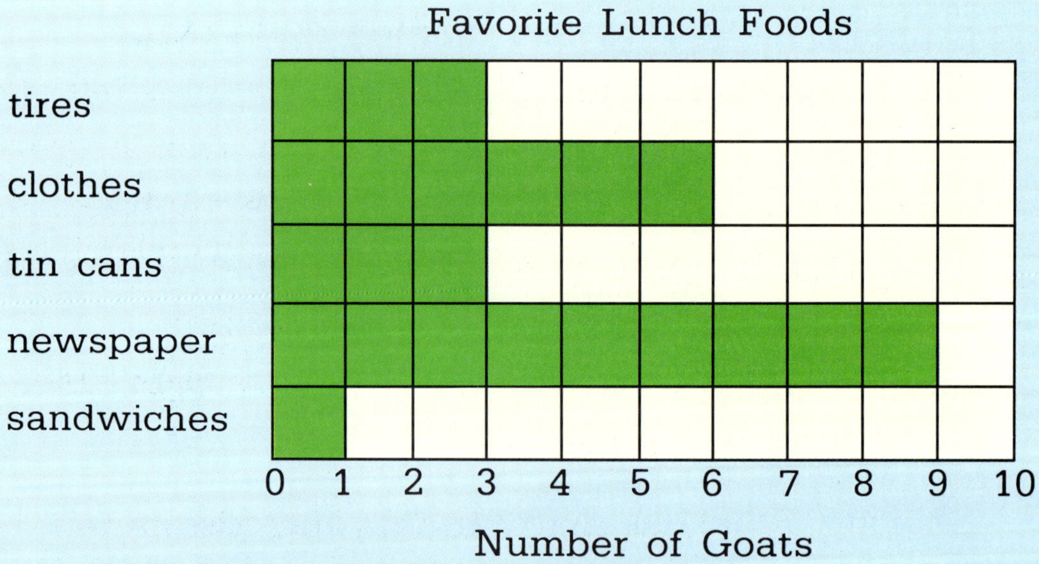

This chart is called a **bar graph**. The title at the top of a bar graph tells you what the graph is about. The title of this bar graph is "Favorite Lunch Foods."

The foods that the goats eat for lunch are listed on the left side of this bar graph. The numbers at the bottom of the bar graph stand for the number of goats that eat each food.

How many goats like to eat clothes for lunch? Look at the bar next to the word *clothes* on the graph. The bar next to *clothes* goes out to the line marked *6*. Six goats like to eat clothes for lunch.

Which food do the most goats like to eat? Find the word next to the longest bar on the graph. *Newspaper* is next to the longest bar, so newspaper must be the food liked by the most goats.

Answer the following questions using the bar graph.

1. How many goats like tin cans?
2. Which two foods are liked by three goats?
3. Which food is the favorite food of only one goat? Who might that goat be?

Old Turtle tells some stories about two very different baseball players. Read to find out what makes Old Turtle's stories the best.

Old Turtle's Baseball Stories

by Leonard Kessler

It was winter—cold, cold winter. Old Turtle sat by the warm wood stove. Owl, Frog, Chicken, and Duck huddled by the stove, too. In the summer they played baseball. But in the winter they told each other . . . baseball stories.

Old Turtle told the best stories.

"Tell us a true baseball story," said Frog.

"Who was the greatest pitcher?" asked Owl.

"The greatest pitcher was Cleo Octopus," Turtle said.

"Great fast ball?" asked Chicken.

"The fastest," said Turtle.

"Good slow ball?" asked Duck.

"The slowest," said Turtle.

"Let me tell you a story about Cleo Octopus."

"It was a very big game. The score was 0-0, top of the sixth. Cleo was the pitcher for the Sea Champs.

" 'Throw your best pitch. I'll knock it out of the park,' the batter yelled.

"Well, Cleo looked at the batter a long time. Then she wound up and threw a fast ball, slow ball, curve ball, and knuckle ball—all at the same time! Swish!

" 'No fair. No fair,' yelled the fans.

" 'You are out!' the umpire shouted."

"The hitter was out?" asked Frog.

"No," said Turtle. "Cleo was out. The umpire tossed her out of the game.

"Cleo quit baseball. She did not want to pitch just one ball at a time."

"What did she do then?" asked Owl.

"She opened a hot dog stand near the ball park. She worked there all by herself. Greatest hot dog pitcher that I ever saw," said Old Turtle.

"Is that a true story?" asked Duck.

"Every word of it," said Turtle.

"Well, who was the greatest hitter?" asked Owl.

"Oh, that's easy. His name was Melvin Moose," said Turtle.

"Righty or lefty?" asked Frog.

"Melvin could hit righty, lefty, and other ways, too!" Turtle told them.

"What other ways?" Duck asked.

"Well, let me tell you a story about Melvin Moose.

"It was a big game. Melvin was at bat. Goose was pitching to Moose. Goose wound up and threw a wild pitch right at Melvin's head."

"And what did Melvin do?" asked Chicken.

"Did he hit the dirt?" asked Owl.

"Did he duck?" asked Duck.

"No," said Turtle. "Melvin pounded that ball with his antlers. Pow!"

"Wow," said Frog.

"It was the start of a new game . . . called Mooseball," Turtle said.

"Is that really true?" asked Duck.

"Every word of it," said Turtle.

"Well, we know who the greatest storyteller is," said Frog.

"Who?" asked Owl.

"Old Turtle!" they all shouted.

Discussing the Selection

1. What made Cleo and Melvin different from other baseball players?
2. Why did the umpire throw Cleo out of the game?
3. How did Melvin invent a new game?
4. Reread the part of the story that told what Cleo did after she left baseball.
5. Why do you think the animals said that Old Turtle was the best storyteller?

Using Language

Writing Baseball Words

Prewriting In the story, the author used some words that are used in the game of baseball. You need to know the meanings of these special words if you want to understand the game.

Guided Writing Write *Baseball Words* at the top of a sheet of paper. Reread the story. As you read, write any baseball words that you find. What is the meaning of each word?

Postwriting With a friend, read your lists of baseball words. Then tell what each word means. Use a dictionary to check each meaning.

Do You Know?

1. Why would a spider make a good outfielder?

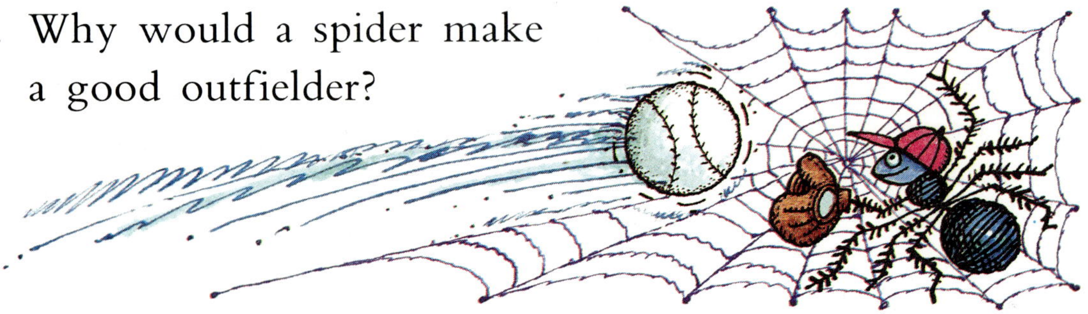

1. It's good at catching flies.

2. Why is a ball park the coolest place?

2. All the fans are in the stands.

3. What do eggs and a losing ball team have in common?

3. They both get beaten.

4. What do a bat and a fly swatter have in common?

4. They both hit flies.

5. What's the biggest jewel in the world?

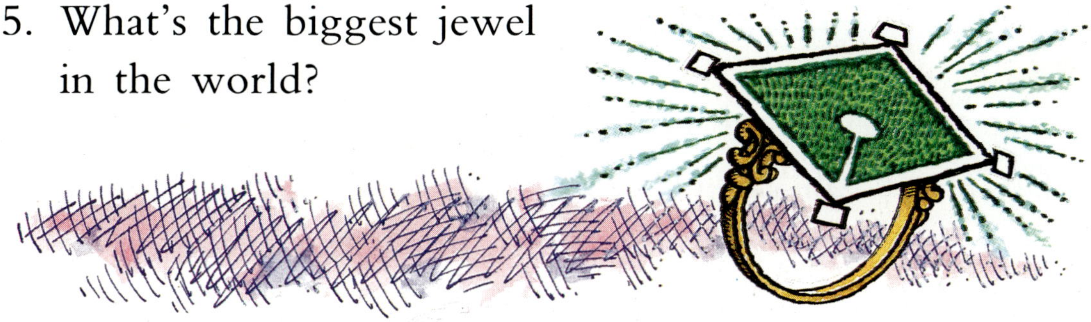

5. A baseball diamond is the biggest jewel.

6. Why was the baseball player arrested?

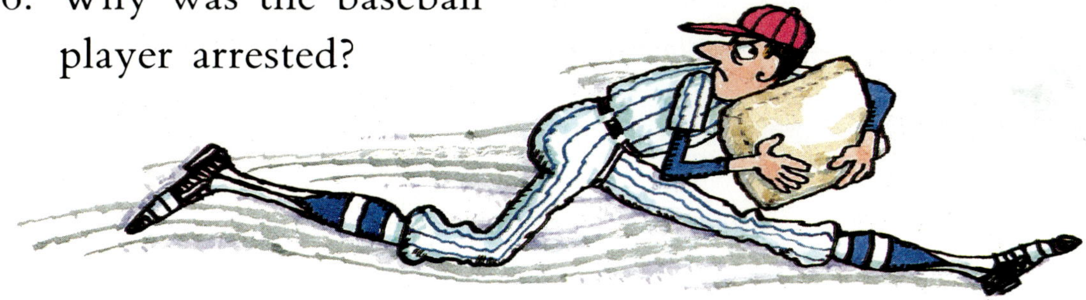

6. He was caught stealing bases.

The octopus is a creature different from any other. Read to find out why.

The Surprising Octopus

by Alice L. Hopf

For thousands of years, most people have been afraid of the octopus. That's probably because its eight legs and large head make it look like a monster.

Octopuses are not monsters at all. In fact, most octopuses are shy creatures, hiding behind rocks or swimming away at the first hint of danger.

There are over 150 kinds of octopuses. Some are no bigger than your hand. Others can grow to be giants that are thirty-five feet wide from the tip of one arm to the tip of another.

Octopuses live in all the oceans of the world. Some live as deep as a mile down. They are found in cold places, as well as warm ones. Octopuses usually live alone. They need only a hole among the rocks in which to hide from their enemies.

There are no bones in the body of an octopus. The head and body are connected without a neck, and the eight arms of an octopus are attached to its head. The octopus has large round eyes on its head.

An octopus has many ways of moving. It can shoot water out of its body and move itself in the opposite direction. Or, it can tiptoe across the sandy bottom of an ocean, using its arms like legs. It can also move using the powerful suckers that are on the underside of each arm. It clamps the suckers onto a rock. Then it pulls its body across the space between itself and the rock.

Suckers are also used to catch animals for food. With its suckers, an octopus can grab hold of a lobster or another animal. The octopus then carves it up and devours the food with its sharp beak.

The octopus has some remarkable ways of escaping from its enemies. If an enemy catches an octopus by one of its arms, the octopus simply lets the arm break off. The octopus then finds a place to hide until a new arm grows.

Another way an octopus can escape is by squirting a black ink-like liquid at an enemy. The cloud of ink blinds the enemy for a moment, allowing the octopus to escape. But the ink that the clever octopus squirts is not just a smoke screen. The cloud of ink is often shaped and colored like an octopus. While the enemy chases the cloud of ink, the octopus changes color and darts off.

Today, scientists study the octopus where it lives in the ocean. One thing they have learned is that the octopus is a clever animal that can deal with many situations.

Discussing the Selection

1. Tell some ways that the octopus is different from other animals.
2. How does an octopus move through water?
3. What are some different ways an octopus escapes from its enemies?
4. How was Cleo Octopus like a real octopus? How was she different?

Using Language

Playing "Ticktacktoe"

Planning See how many facts you remember from "The Surprising Octopus" by playing the game "ticktacktoe."

Working Together Get together with a friend. On a sheet of paper, make a grid like the one below.

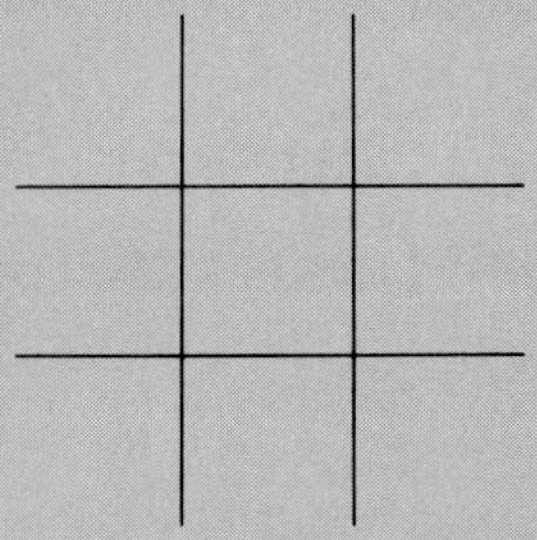

Decide whose mark will be *O* and whose mark will be *X*. Take turns asking each other questions from the story. When a player answers correctly, that player may make his or her mark in the grid. The first player to get three *O*'s or three *X*'s in a row is the winner.

Sharing Change partners and play the game again.

(To be read by the teacher)

The Octopus

. . .

He's scary to look at, but never attacks,
Just huddles in caves among underwater rocks,
And if he's discovered, he's too scared to think
But clouds up the water with great swirls of ink

And scuttles away in an eight-legged hurry
To some other cave, where he sits full of worry
And hopes no one finds him, with which I agree.
If someone *must* find him, I hope it's not me.

John Gardner

A little girl must find a different way to get a birthday present for her grandfather. What will she do?

Josefina February

by Evaline Ness

Not long ago on a high hill in Haiti, there lived a little girl named Josefina February. Josefina lived with her grandfather, Mr. February, in a house with bamboo walls and a banana leaf roof.

In back of Josefina's house was a grove. In the grove, all kinds of fruits and vegetables and flowers were growing.

Early every morning, Josefina and her grandfather picked the fruit and carried it in baskets on their heads to sell at the marketplace. They lived on the money they got from the fruit. But Mr. February always gave Josefina a penny or two to spend as she pleased.

One morning, instead of going to the market, Josefina's grandfather went to work all day in Mr. Hippolyte's sugar cane fields.

It was her grandfather's birthday, and Josefina wanted to buy him a pair of real leather shoes. If she could sell one basket of fruit, she would easily have enough money, with the pennies she had saved, to buy the shoes.

After her grandfather left, Josefina went to the grove. While she was busily picking fruit, she heard a strange sound. Josefina looked behind a nearby bush and saw a little black burro clumsily trying to stand. He had a fringe of brown hair on top of his head that looked like a cap.

Josefina picked up the burro and held him close. She decided to call him Cap. She wondered if Cap belonged to someone. How she wished he belonged to her! She would teach him clever tricks. She would play games with him. And when he was older, she would ride on his back to the sea.

Josefina was so busy daydreaming, it was noon before she remembered the fruit she had picked to take to the market. She decided to take Cap with her.

Then she had a thought. What if Cap belonged to the very first person she met? If Cap belonged to someone else, he couldn't belong to her.

But perhaps the burro was like Josefina, who had no mother, no father, no sister, no brother. Cap might not even have a grandfather. Somehow she felt warmer, so she put her basket on her head, picked up Cap, and started down the hill.

The first person Josefina met was Lilly. "Pardon me, Lilly," Josefina said. "Does this burro belong to you?"

Lilly swept by nastily without a word. Josefina whispered to Cap, "Well, anyway, it wasn't the first person."

Josefina smiled and went on. Soon, she saw a woman with three blackbirds. When Josefina asked her if she had lost a baby burro, the woman didn't say a word. But the three blackbirds cackled and croaked, "*Not we not we not we!*"

Josefina hugged Cap and hurried on to the marketplace. But when Josefina got to the marketplace, it was empty!

All the people had packed up and gone home to supper. Josefina didn't know what to do. She was happy and sad at the same time. Now Cap belonged to her, but she had no real leather shoes to give to her grandfather for his birthday.

Josefina turned away from the empty marketplace and started to walk home. As she passed Mr. Hippolyte's sugar-cane fields, she heard her name called. It was Mr. Hippolyte himself.

Josefina tried to smile, but instead she started to cry. Mr. Hippolyte just waited. At last, Josefina wiped away her tears and told him her story.

Mr. Hippolyte looked at Josefina for a long time. Then he said, "It just happens that I have a new pair of real leather shoes. Would you like to trade Cap for the shoes?"

It was Josefina's turn to look at Mr. Hippolyte for a long time. Then she nodded her head. She was afraid to speak for fear she would cry again.

While she waited for Mr. Hippolyte to return with the shoes, Josefina made two neat braids in Cap's mane and tied them with the ribbons from her hair. She kissed Cap's nose and told him to be good. She promised Cap she would never, never forget him.

When Josefina got home, it was almost dark. She cooked ham and yams and cut up all the fruit from her basket.

Josefina had just put the new shoes on the table when her grandfather walked in. He stood and smiled at Josefina, and Josefina smiled back. Then Mr. February put on his real leather shoes and kissed Josefina on top of her head.

Mr. February and Josefina ate the birthday supper. They had almost finished when Mr. February said, "Poor Mr. Hippolyte. He has a big responsibility, and he thinks he cannot handle it alone. He wondered if you would like to take care of it for him."

Before Josefina could say a word, the door slowly opened. In wobbled a little black burro, fringed on top, with ribbons in his mane.

Discussing the Selection

1. How did Josefina get the shoes for her grandfather?
2. Why was Josefina late getting to the marketplace?
3. What happened when Josefina met Mr. Hippolyte?
4. Where in the story did you find out that Mr. Hippolyte was a kind man?
5. What are some words you might use to describe Josefina?

Using Language

Writing About Josefina

Prewriting Josefina February lived in a faraway place called Haiti. In some ways, Josefina's life was the same as yours, but in other ways it was different.

Writing With a friend, reread "Josefina February." Write some sentences that tell how Josefina's life was the same as yours. Then write some sentences that tell how Josefina's life was different.

Postwriting Get together with another group and share your lists. Find and read the parts of the story that gave you the ideas for your sentences.

Let's Act It Out

A **play** is a story that has been written to be acted out or performed. You may read a play to yourself just as you would a story. Or your class may read a play together, with a different person taking the part of each character.

The characters in a play are called the **cast**. When a play is performed, the lines of each character in the cast are read by a different person.

The **setting** tells where the play takes place. The setting of the play that follows is a cabin on a mountaintop in Ireland.

A play is made up of lines that the characters say. Look at the following line from a play:

> **John:** He says that there's water right out front under those two rocks.

John is the name of the character who is speaking. The name is printed in **boldface**. The words that John is to say come after the two dots called a colon. The person who is taking the part of John should read only the words that follow the colon.

Words in parentheses sometimes follow a character's name. These words are called **stage directions.** Stage directions may tell how a line is to be read. Or they may tell what the actors are to do as the line is said. For example:

> **John** *(opening the door):* Good day, ladies.

The words in parentheses are the stage directions. What should the person playing the part of John be doing as he or she says the line?

Look for the cast, the setting, and the stage directions when you read a play. This information will help you understand what is happening.

Grannie and her friends come up the mountain to visit the McCools. Read to find out the news that they bring.

Finn McCool

by May Lynch

THE CAST

Finn McCool	**Grannie**
Una McCool	**Mrs. Shane**
	Mrs. Finnerty
	Cuhullin

Owen
John
Jamie } ***the children***
Meg
Kellie

Setting: ***Finn McCool's*** *cabin, on top of Knockmany Mountain, in Ireland.*

ACT I

(***Una** is at the washtub, wringing out some laundry.* ***Owen, Jamie,** and **John** are sitting nearby.*)

Una: That's the last of the washing, and I must say it was a big one!

Owen: I'll say. I carried six buckets of water up Knockmany Mountain this morning.

Una: I'll be glad when your father finds us a spring near the house.

John: He says that there's water right out front under those two rocks.

Jamie: Yes, and he's going to move them someday.

Owen: But *someday* never comes.

Una: Don't speak that way of your father. After all, the dear man is very busy and tired. (***Meg*** *and* ***Kellie*** *enter.*)

Kellie: Mother! Mother! Guess what!

Meg: Grannie, Mrs. Finnerty, and Mrs. Shane are coming up the mountain.

Una: Your grannie hasn't been here in a long time. Help me tidy up the room.

Kellie (*at window*): Here they are.

John (*opening the door*): Good day, ladies.

Grannie: Well, I must say, that mountain gets steeper every year.

Mrs. Finnerty: And that wind gets stronger and stronger.

Mrs. Shane: Una, however do you stand it up here?

Una (*laughing*): Finn McCool wouldn't live anywhere else in the world, and neither would I.

Grannie: Where is Finn today?

John: He's somewhere about. He's busy, I guess.

Una: He's such a busy man, you know.

Mrs. Shane: It's too bad he's too busy to find a spring up here. Your children shouldn't have to carry water up the mountain.

John: We really like to do that, Mrs. Shane. Besides, our father says that someday he is going to let my brothers and me help him split open those rocks out there. There's water under them. (*Ladies shake their heads.*)

Meg: Grannie, Ladies, do sit down and have a cup of tea.

Grannie: It's good to see you, Una. Since Finn built this house up here, we seldom get together.

Mrs. Shane: Is it true that Finn came up here to get away from Cuhullin?

Una: Goodness, no.

John: Who is Cuhullin?

Mrs. Shane: He's a giant. That's who he is.

John: Our father is a giant, too.

Mrs. Shane: Oh, but Cuhullin is very strong. He's beaten every single giant in Ireland except Finn McCool, and Cuhullin can't find him.

Mrs. Finnerty: There's talk that he's on his way here to find Finn.

Mrs. Shane: Yes, they say he'll stamp Finn into pancakes when he finds him.

John: But why?

Grannie: It's a long story, John, but I'll make it brief. Finn used to brag about how much stronger he was than Cuhullin. Cuhullin heard about it, and so he began to look for Finn McCool.

Una: We have nothing to be afraid of. Finn will take care of us.

Grannie: Please, come stay with me.

Una: No, we'll be perfectly safe. (*thinks for a moment*) But I just remembered I must do some baking.

(***Una*** *starts to mix flour and salt in a bowl, as* ***Grannie*** *and other ladies rise.*)

Grannie: Well, we'll be on our way then.

Una: Must you go so soon, ladies? (*Ladies nod and start toward door.*) Finn will be sorry he wasn't here to see you. Come again soon.

Mrs. Finnerty: We will, Una. (*to Grannie*) Poor Finn McCool will be no more. Poor Finn McCool. (*They leave.*)

Discussing the Selection

1. What news did the ladies bring?
2. Why does Cuhullin want to stamp Finn into pancakes?
3. How did Una react to what the ladies told her?
4. Find and read the part of the story where Mrs. Finnerty showed she feared for Finn McCool's life.
5. What do you think will happen next in the story?

Using Language

Making Predictions

Planning Think about the characters you have met so far in the play. What characters might be in the second act of the play that weren't in the first? What might happen to them?

Working Together With two friends, make predictions about what might happen in the second act of the play. Tell why you made each prediction. Reread the first act again if you need information to support your prediction.

Sharing Share your predictions with another group and tell why you made each prediction. Listen as the other group tells its predictions. Were any of the predictions the same?

Read to find out the different ways that Una plans to outsmart Cuhullin.

Finn McCool

by May Lynch

ACT 2

(***Una** is busy covering two iron skillets with bread dough.*)

Kellie: Mother, do you believe what the ladies said about Cuhullin—that he will stamp Father into pancakes?

Una: Don't worry about it. One bite of this bread with a skillet in it will take care of Cuhullin. (***Finn** comes in.*)

Finn: I'm a dead man. I've been to town, and the giant Cuhullin is looking for me. He told someone he'd squeeze me into a sausage.

Girls: Is he big?

Finn: Too big for me to handle. And *I'm* too big to hide from him.

Una: Just leave everything to me, Finn. I'll handle Cuhullin. Get that long nightgown of mine and find an old baby's bonnet. Put them on and hide in that bed over there.

Finn: Right here? Hide here in this bed out in the open?

(***Una*** *nods.* ***Finn*** *goes out and comes back wearing a long white nightgown and a bonnet. He climbs into bed.*)

Una: Girls, go get Jamie and Owen and go to the tip of the mountain and watch for Cuhullin. John, you go, too. As soon as you see Cuhullin coming up the mountain, let out a long loud whistle.

Finn: Oh! Oh! I'm scared. Cuhullin will squash me like a mosquito.

Una: Nonsense! You just listen to my plan. I've already made bread Cuhullin will never forget. Now I will take a stone and make it look like cheese.

(*A loud whistle is heard.*)

Una: Cuhullin is coming! Now keep the bonnet on and remember *who* you are. (*She hands* ***Finn*** *a stone and a round cheese from the table. A loud banging at the door is heard.*)

Cuhullin: Open up, Finn McCool. (***Una*** *opens the door, looking surprised.*)

Una: Come in, stranger.

Cuhullin: Is Finn McCool home?

Una: Dear me, no! He left here a little while ago. Someone said a giant named Cuhullin was down in town looking for him. Finn went right down to make pancakes out of him.

Cuhullin: I'm Cuhullin.

Una: Oh, you poor man. Finn has a bad temper. Don't let him find you.

Cuhullin: I've been looking for him for years.

Una: Well, wait for him then. But don't say I didn't warn you.

Cuhullin: I'll wait.

Una: Would you do me a favor while you wait? Would you turn the house around? Finn always turns it around in the fall when the wind blows at the door. It makes the house warmer in winter.

Cuhullin: Turn the house? Nothing easier. (*He goes outside and easily lifts up the house.* ***Finn*** *looks at the ceiling and groans.* ***Cuhullin*** *comes back in.*)

Una: Thank you very much. Now would you do something else? Finn has been meaning to pull those rocks apart and find us a spring, but he hurried off, and I do need water. (***Cuhullin*** *goes out. A loud crash is heard.*)

Una (*to* ***Finn***): Goodness! He pulled apart those rocks with his bare hands and made a spring! (***Finn*** *groans.* ***Cuhullin*** *comes back.*)

Cuhullin: What now?

Una: Why don't you come and have a bite to eat? Here's a cup of hot tea and some warm bread. (***Cuhullin*** *bites into the bread.*)

Cuhullin: By thunder! I just broke my two front teeth! What did you give me to eat?

Una: Only what Finn eats. He and our little baby in the bed eat this bread all the time.

(***Una*** *takes a loaf of bread to* ***Finn****, who pretends to eat it.*)

Cuhullin: I'd like to see that child. He must be some boy!

Una: Get up, dearie, and show the man that you're Finn's little son.

Finn (*jumping out of bed*): Are you strong? Can you squeeze water from a stone? My father can, and so can I. (*He hands a stone to **Cuhullin** who tries to squeeze water from it.*) Ah, you can't do it.

(***Finn** exchanges the stone for the cheese without **Cuhullin** seeing it. Then he squeezes the cheese until water drips from it.*)

Finn: My father showed me how to squeeze water from cheese. He can stamp a man into pancakes.

Una: Get into bed, Son. You'll never grow strong and big like your father if you don't get your rest.

Cuhullin (*looking scared*): I think I'd better go before Finn comes back!

(***Cuhullin*** *runs out.* ***Finn*** *sighs with relief.* ***Una*** *laughs. The children come running in.*)

Meg: Mother, what did you do to Cuhullin?

John: He was holding his jaw and crying about some broken teeth.

Owen: He said something about pancakes and a baby giant.

Finn: Ah, your mother is very clever. She made stones look like cheese.

Una: Your father fooled him. Cuhullin thought your father was squeezing water from a stone. Finn really squeezed water from cheese.

Finn: And your mother put iron skillets into her bread.

Una: But your Father fooled him by pretending to nibble around the crust.

Owen: Why are you wearing that silly outfit, Father?

Una: Oh, you should have seen how your father fooled Cuhullin by pretending to be a baby giant. (*Everyone laughs.*)

Finn: Now, if I can just get out of this nightgown, I'll lie down and have a rest. A busy man like me gets very tired.

Discussing the Selection

1. How did Una outsmart Cuhullin?
2. Why was Finn afraid of Cuhullin?
3. What happened after Finn squeezed water from the cheese?
4. Where in the story did you first know that Una's plan would work?
5. What do you think would have happened if Una hadn't been so clever?

Using Language

Describing Characters

Prewriting Think about Finn and Una. What are some words you might use to describe each character? Make one list of words that describe Finn and one list of words that describe Una.

Guided Writing Find the parts of the play that help to explain why you chose the words you did. Make a note of where each part is next to each word you chose.

Postwriting Share your lists with two other friends. Using the parts of the play you noted, explain why you chose each word.

(To be read by the teacher)

The Giant

I used to have a dream
long ago
about a giant
tall as a tree.

He came to the door
and said, "Come,"
holding his hand to me.

I never went
but now that I'm bigger
I wish I had.
He may have been a friendly giant
and I made him sad.

Charlotte Zolotow

UNIT CLOSER

A DIFFERENT WAY

The stories in this unit were about characters who behaved in ways different than you might have expected. Tell who these characters were and what made their behavior different.

Then answer the following questions:

1. Gregory was different from other goats. What made Finn McCool different from other giants?

2. List some words that would describe both Cleo Octopus and a real octopus.

3. You read the play "Finn McCool." Which other story in this unit would make a good play? How would the story need to be changed?

4. Which characters were satisfied with the way things turned out at the end of each story? Why? Which characters were not satisfied? Why?

5. Mr. Hippolyte had a clever way of returning the burro to Josefina. What did other characters in this unit do that you thought was clever?

Bibliography

Books in This Unit

Old Turtle's Baseball Stories by Leonard Kessler. Greenwillow, 1982.

Dramatized Folktales of the World by May Lynch. Plays Inc., 1971.

Josefina February by Evaline Ness. Scribner's, 1963.

Gregory, the Terrible Eater by Mitchell Sharmat. Four Winds Press, 1980.

Additional Books to Read

Octopus by Carol Carrick. Houghton Mifflin, 1978.

Fin M'Coul, The Giant of Knockmany Hill by Tomie de Paola. Holiday, 1982.

Georgia Music by Helen V. Griffith. Greenwillow, 1986.

The Purple Coat by Amy Hest. Four Winds Press, 1986.

Alexander and the Wind-up Mouse by Leo Lionni. Pantheon, 1969.

UNIT 4

MAKING PLANS

Making plans can be a lot of fun. You might plan a trip with your family, or a surprise birthday party for a friend, or a picnic in the park. Each of the stories in this unit is about making plans and carrying them out.

In the first story, a girl comes to America from Vietnam, and her new classmates plan to do something special for her. In the selection that follows, you'll read about some children who live in the north and how they have fun. The next story tells about how the Sun and the Moon make plans for the arrival of a guest. Then a clever crow plans how he will get a drink of water from a pitcher. Next, you'll learn about water and how it behaves by doing some experiments. Finally, you'll find out why the people of a town decide not to stick to a plan they make.

As you read each selection, think about the following questions: What plans are made? Do the plans work out?

Everyone in Ut's family, except for her mother, has come to America from Vietnam. How does Ut's class plan to help her see her mother?

Angel Child, Dragon Child

by Michele Maria Surat

My sisters skipped through the stone gate two by two. Mother was not there to skip with me. Mother was far away in Vietnam. She could not say, "Ut, my little one, be an Angel Child. Be happy in your new American school."

I hugged the wall and peeked around the corner.

A boy with fire-colored hair pointed his finger. "Pajamas!" he shouted. "They wore white pajamas to school!" The American children tilted back their long noses, laughing.

I turned away. "I want to go home to Father."

My sister Chi Hai's hands curved over my shoulders. "Children stay where parents place them, Ut. We stay."

Somewhere, a loud bell jangled. I lost my sisters in a swirl of rushing children.

Inside, the children did not sit together and chant as I was taught. Instead, they waved their hands and said their lessons one by one. I hid my hands, but the teacher called my name. "Nguyen Hoa."

Hoa is my true name, but I am Ut. Ut is my at-home name—a tender name for smallest daughter.

"Hoa," the teacher said slowly. "Write your name, please."

"I not understand," I whispered. The other children giggled. I stood and bowed like an Angel Child. The children screeched like bluejays.

I sat down and flipped up my desk top, hiding my angry Dragon face.

Deep in my pocket, I felt Mother's gift—a small wooden matchbox with silvery edges. When I opened the matchbox, I saw Mother's face.

"I will keep you safe in here, Mother," I told her.

Her listening face smiled. In my heart, I heard her voice. "Do not be angry, my smallest daughter," she said. "Be my brave little Dragon."

So all day I was brave, even when the children whispered behind their hands. Finally, the bell rang. Time for home!

In this way, many days passed.

One day at school, small feathers floated past the frosty windows. "Mother," I whispered, "this is snow. It makes everything soft, even the angry trees with no leaves to make them pretty."

My fingers danced on the desk top while I waited for the bell. When it rang, I rushed out the door.

Outside, snowflakes left wet kisses on my cheeks. "Chi Hai, catch some!" I called.

"It disappears!" she cried.

Just as Chi Hai spoke, a snowball stung her chin. That red-haired boy darted behind a maple tree. He was laughing hard.

I tried, but I could not be a noble Dragon. Before I knew it, I was scooping up snow. My hands burned, and my fingers turned red. I threw my snowball, and the laughing stopped.

Suddenly, the boy tackled me! We rolled in the snow, kicking and yelling, until the principal's large hand pinched my shoulder.

"Inside!" he said, and he marched us to our classroom.

"We can't have this fighting. You two have to help each other," ordered the principal. He pointed at me. "Hoa, you need to speak to Raymond. Use our words. Tell him about Vietnam." Raymond glared. "And you, Raymond, must learn to listen. You will write Hoa's story."

The principal turned and left the room.

Across the room, I heard a sniffle. I crept over. Gently, I tugged the sad boy's sleeve. He didn't move. "Raymond," I pleaded, "not cry. I give you cookie."

Suddenly, his head bounced up. "Hoa!" he shouted. "You said my name. You didn't use funny words." He broke off a piece of the cookie.

"I say English," I answered proudly. "And you call me Ut. Ut is my at-home name, from Vietnam."

"Okay, Ut," he said. "But only if you tell me what's in your matchbox."

"My mother," I told him. We giggled and ate the cookie crumbs.

Then Raymond asked, "Why do you need your mother's picture?"

"Mother is far away," I said softly.

"She didn't come with you?"

"No money for Mother to come," I sighed.

"Wait," said Raymond. He grabbed a pencil. I handed him a sheet of paper. "Now tell me about Vietnam," he said.

Raymond wrote my words, and I drew pictures. When we were ready, Raymond leaned out the door. "Done!" he beamed. He waved the story like a flag.

The principal walked up the hall. "You may go," said the big man.

We dashed through the stone gate together.

The next day, the principal read our story to the whole school. "These girls left their country and sailed many oceans to be here. They left behind their home, their friends, and most important of all, their mother. So now . . ."

"Ut's mother needs money for the long boat ride to America!" shouted Raymond. "We could have a fair and earn the money."

I hid my eyes. I held my breath. Chi Hai squeezed my hand.

"A special fair! A fair that is all about Vietnam!" my teacher exclaimed. My eyes opened wide.

"But who will help with the fair?" asked the principal.

"We will!" squealed the children.

"Well, what are we waiting for?" said the principal.

On the special day, I was the hostess. I wore my white dress from Vietnam. I welcomed everyone to our fair and bowed like an Angel Child.

High above our heads, our rainbow dragon floated freely. Below, Chi Hai and her friends wore aprons and sold rice cakes and cookies. Raymond popped balloons and won three goldfish.

By the end of the day, we had just enough money to send to Mother. "When will she come?" I wondered.

Every day, we walked home wondering, "When will Mother come?"

We slid through icy winter. . . .

We splashed through spring rain. . . .

We tiptoed barefoot through the grass. . . .

On the last day of school, Raymond and I raced home faster than all my sisters. We were the first to see Father at the picture window and beside him . . . Mother!

Discussing the Selection

1. What plan did Ut's class have to help her see her mother again?
2. Why didn't Ut's mother come to America with the rest of her family?
3. What happened when the principal read Ut's story to the rest of the school?
4. Find and read the part of the story that gave you an idea of how long Ut had to wait for her mother to come.
5. Why do you think Ut's classmates made fun of her at first?

Using Language

Welcoming a New Classmate

Planning Imagine that Ut is a new student in your class. Think about some ways you could make her feel welcome.

Working Together Get together with a partner and talk about how you would help Ut feel welcome in your class. What are some things you could do to help her feel at home? What are some things you could learn from Ut?

Sharing Share your ideas and those of your partner with two other classmates. How many of your ideas are the same? If there is a new student in your class, use your ideas to help him or her feel welcome.

COMPREHENSION/
THINKING SKILL

What's Happening?

When you read a story, do you try to guess what will happen? When you guess what will happen, you are **making a prediction.** Whether you are right or wrong, making predictions is an important part of reading.

Read the sentences below from "Angel Child, Dragon Child." In this part, Ut sees Raymond do something mean.

> Just as Chi Hai spoke, a snowball stung her chin. That red-haired boy darted behind a maple tree. He was laughing hard.

What did you think Ut would do? You probably guessed that Ut would be angry at Raymond. So it wasn't hard to predict that Ut would get into a snowball fight with Raymond.

Read the following paragraph:

> Ben was cleaning out his closet. What a mess! As he worked, Ben made two stacks. In one stack, he put things like worn-out socks, broken toys, and old school papers. In the other stack, he put shirts that were too small, games that he didn't want any more, and an old baseball mitt.

What will Ben do with each of the stacks? More than likely, Ben will throw away the first stack. What will he do with the things in the second stack? Will he give them to his little brother? Or will he sell them? Either prediction is a good one. Both are based on what you read and what you know about how people get rid of things they no longer want.

When you read a story, try to predict what will happen. Making predictions can be fun and will help you understand what is going on in the story.

The Yukon covers a huge area in the northwest corner of Canada. Read to find out some of the special things the children of the Yukon do.

Children of the Yukon

by Ted Harrison

It was a cloudless summer day back in 1968 when Ted Harrison arrived in the Yukon. He had been hired to teach school. From the day he arrived, he knew that he was in a special place.

Since that day in 1968, Ted Harrison has become the Yukon's best-known painter. Many of his paintings are of the children of the Yukon. Some of his paintings of Yukon children show them doing things other children do. But most of his paintings show Yukon children doing things that children farther south never have a chance to do.

Winter and night come early to the Yukon. In November, by mid-afternoon, darkness has already fallen. The bold and noisy ravens have returned from their summer nesting places. Children make snowmen on their way home from school. Soon, the very dry cold will make the snow too powdery for packing.

Fishing as well as trapping goes on in the winter. Children help their fathers fish through the ice on lakes in the Yukon.

The snowshoe rabbit is trapped for food and fur—to make mukluks and mittens. These things keep the people of the Yukon warm during the long, hard winter.

The sounds of dogs barking and children laughing often mean there is a snowshoe race. Running on snowshoes is difficult but fun. Even beginners laugh at themselves as they trip and tumble and struggle to get back up.

In the Yukon, every family seems to own a canoe or boat. As soon as the last ice leaves the lakes and rivers, there is a great rush toward the water. Everyone wants to enjoy the long days of the short summer.

"Joyous Summer Day Festival" is a celebration held each year by the native people in the village of Tagish. Families come from all around to dance and sing around a blazing campfire. Moose meat and fish are served.

Ted Harrison has visited most of the villages in the Yukon and has seen some of its wilderness. During his travels, he has also gotten to know many of the Yukon people. His paintings let the rest of the world know these special people, too.

Discussing the Selection

1. What are some special things that children of the Yukon do?
2. What are some things that children of the Yukon do that other children do, too?
3. What might a Yukon family plan to do in the summer?
4. In 1968, Ted Harrison went to the Yukon to teach. What might he have had in common with Ut, who came to America in "Angel Child, Dragon Child"?

Using Language

Writing Descriptions

Prewriting Pretend that you work for a travel club. Your job is to get people interested in visiting the Yukon. What are some different things that people of the Yukon do that seem like fun? What are some things in the Yukon that visitors might be interested in seeing?

Writing Use what you know from the selection to help you make a travel booklet about the Yukon. Draw pictures that show the people of the Yukon doing special things. Then write some sentences describing each picture. Make a cover for your booklet.

Sharing Share your travel booklet with other friends. Talk about what you would like to see and do if you ever travel to the Yukon.

(To be read by the teacher)

Eskimo Chant

There is joy in
Feeling the warmth
Come to the great world
And seeing the sun
Follow its old footprints
In the summer night.

There is fear in
Feeling the cold
Come to the great world
And seeing the moon
—Now new moon, now full moon—
Follow its old footprints
In the winter night.

Translated by *Knud Rasmussen*

Grouping Things That Are Alike

Some things can be grouped together by how they are alike. Grouping things that are alike is called **classifying**.

Look at the two groups of animal names listed below. The animals are grouped, or classified, by where they live.

Land Animals	Water Animals
dogs	whales
horses	octopuses
cows	dolphins

The name given to each group is called a **heading.** Under which heading would you classify a tiger? Under which heading would you classify a goldfish? Under which heading would you classify a moose?

An author will sometimes classify things so that it will be easier for readers to remember what they've read.

Read the following paragraph that tells some things that Yukon children do.

> During part of the year, the children make snowmen, go ice fishing, and learn how to snowshoe. When the days are longer, they go out in boats, pick berries, and go camping.

The author classified the activities in the paragraph into two groups. First he told what Yukon children do in the winter. Then he told what they do in the summer.

Make a chart like the one below. Fill in the chart using information from the paragraph.

Summer	Winter

The Sun and the Moon make plans to build a bigger house so that the Water can come and visit. Will the new house be big enough?

Why the Sun and the Moon Live in the Sky

by Elphinstone Dayrell

Many years ago, the Sun and the Water were great friends and both lived on the earth together. The Sun often visited the Water, but the Water never returned his visits.

The Sun was distraught by this, so one day he asked the Water why he never came to visit.

The Water replied that the Sun's house was not big enough. The Water then said, "If you wish me to visit you, you must build a bigger house. But I warn you that it will have to be a very large place, for my water animals take up a lot of room."

The Sun promised to build a very large house. Soon afterwards, he returned to his wife, the Moon, who greeted him with a broad smile. The Sun told the Moon what he had promised the Water.

The next day, the Sun and the Moon began building a large house in which to entertain their friend. When the house was completed, the Sun and the Moon asked the Water to visit them.

When the Water arrived, one of the water animals called out to the Sun and asked whether it would be safe for the Water to enter. The Sun answered, "Yes, tell my friend to come in."

The Water began to flow in, along with the fish and all the water animals.

Very soon the Water was knee-deep, so the Water asked the Sun if it was still safe. The Sun again said yes, so more of the water animals came in.

When the Water was level with the top of a man's head, the Water asked the Sun, "Do you think more of my animals ought to come in?"

And the Sun and the Moon both answered yes, not knowing any better. So the Water flowed on and brought more of his animals, until the Sun and the Moon had to perch themselves on top of the roof.

Again the Water addressed the Sun. The Sun gave the same answer, so more of the animals rushed in.

The Water very soon overflowed the top of the roof. The Sun and the Moon were forced to go into the sky, where they have remained ever since.

Discussing the Selection

1. Was the new house big enough for the Water? Explain your answer.
2. Why hadn't the Water ever visited the Sun and the Moon?
3. What happened each time the Water asked if more of his animals should come in?
4. Find the place where the Sun and the Moon first had to leave their house.
5. If you had been the Sun or the Moon, how would you have handled the Water's visit?

Using Language

Explaining Things

Planning "Why the Sun and the Moon Live in the Sky" is an old African folk tale. Long ago, people tried to explain things they didn't understand, so they made up "why" stories. Read the following story titles:

"Why the Stars Are in the Sky"
"Why the Sun Hides Behind Clouds"
"Why There Is Thunder"

Working Together With a partner, choose one of the story titles above or make up one of your own. Tell each other a story like people did long ago to explain things they didn't understand. Your partner may ask questions, and you may make up more parts to your story.

Sharing Tell your stories to the class.

(To be read by the teacher)

Why the Sky Is Blue

I don't suppose you happen to know
Why the sky is blue? It's because the snow
Takes out the white. That leaves it clean
For the trees and grass to take out the green.
Then pears and bananas start to mellow,
And bit by bit they take out the yellow.
The sunsets, of course, take out the red
And pour it into the ocean bed
Or behind the mountains in the west.
You take all that out and the rest
Couldn't be anything else but blue.

—Look for yourself. You can see it's true.

John Ciardi

A crow wants to drink some water from the bottom of a pitcher. How does he plan to get to the water?

The Crow and the Pitcher

a fable

by Aesop

A big crow had been flying for many miles. He was tired and oh, so thirsty! The day was warm, and in his travels, the crow had passed no rivers or streams or lakes.

"I must find water," thought the crow, "or surely I will die."

At that moment he saw the pitcher. It stood quite alone on the ground by a rock. The crow flew up to it. "Maybe," he hoped, "just maybe it is full of water."

The crow looked inside the pitcher. How happy he was to see that there *was* water in it! Eagerly, he leaned his head in to drink. But alas, his attempt was for naught. The water was at the bottom of the pitcher, and the poor crow could not reach it. He was too big to fit into the pitcher. And he was too short to reach the water at its bottom.

The crow stooped and he strained. He fought and he struggled. But, no matter how hard he tried, his beak never came near the water.

"Hmmm," thought the crow. "I'll have to try something else."

He decided to overturn the pitcher. Even if the water spilled out, he might still get a little of it.

So the crow pushed and he pulled. He tugged and he leaned, but the pitcher was too heavy. He wasn't strong enough to overturn it.

"I must get that water!" said the crow to himself.

As the crow looked around, he saw a pile of small pebbles. This gave him an idea. One by one, the crow picked up the pebbles and cast them into the pitcher. With each pebble, the water in the pitcher rose just a little.

In time, the pebbles caused the water to rise to the top, and the thirsty crow drank his fill.

Much pleased with himself, the crow lay down to take a rest. He had done with his wits what he could not do with force.

Discussing the Selection

1. How did the crow get the water?
2. Why couldn't the crow just drink the water from the pitcher?
3. What finally made the crow think of a way to get the water?
4. Find and read the parts of the story that showed the crow was not a quitter.
5. What do you think is the meaning of the last sentence of the story?

Using Language

Writing a Fable

Prewriting A fable is a story with a hidden lesson. In "The Crow and the Pitcher," the crow had to think of a plan and then work hard to get a drink. What lesson do you think the fable taught? Think of a lesson you might want someone to learn.

Writing Get together with a group and talk about a fable you could write together. Write the fable by taking turns and adding sentences. Keep in mind the lesson you want to teach.

Sharing Add your fable to a class book called "Our Fables." Read a fable that another group wrote.

The crow's plan to raise the level of the water worked. Read to find out why.

Finding Out About Water

by Carol Peske

In "The Crow and the Pitcher," the crow made the level of the water rise by dropping pebbles into the pitcher. Did you know that the pebbles would make the water rise?

Try the following experiments to find out some things about water. Read each experiment first so that you will know what materials to gather and what steps to follow.

EXPERIMENT 1

Materials

1 glass

10 pebbles

water

Fill the glass halfway with water. Drop the pebbles one by one into the water. What happens to the level of the water? It rises a little as each pebble is added.

Do you know why? The pebbles sink to the bottom of the glass and take up space. The water that was at the bottom of the glass moves up, so the water level rises. The pebbles take the place of, or displace, the water that was at the bottom of the glass.

EXPERIMENT 2

Materials

4 glasses	5 rubber bands
1 cork	10 nails
10 coins	water

Fill each glass halfway with water. Then drop the cork into the first glass, the rubber bands into the second glass, the coins into the third glass, and the nails into the fourth glass. Which objects float? Which objects sink?

Put the information on a chart like the one below.

Float	Sink

Which objects made the water level rise when added to the glasses? Under which heading on the chart are those objects listed?

EXPERIMENT 3

Materials

ice-cube tray | water
freezer

Fill an ice-cube tray to the very top with water. Then place the tray in a freezer. After the water is frozen, take a close look at the ice cubes.

You will see that the top of each ice cube goes over the rim of the tray. Do you know why? The reason is that ice, or frozen water, takes up more space than water that is not frozen.

After doing experiments, good scientists always write what they have learned. Write what you have learned from doing each of the experiments in this selection.

Discussing the Selection

1. Why did the water level rise when the crow added pebbles to the pitcher?
2. What did you learn from doing the experiment with the ice-cube tray?
3. What should you always do first when you plan to do an experiment?
4. What other things could the crow have added to the pitcher to make the water level rise?

Using Language

Making a Chart

Prewriting All living things—people, animals, flowers, plants—need water. Think about how you use water every day.

Writing On a sheet of paper, make a chart like the one below. Then list the ways you use water in each place.

Home	School	Outside

Sharing With a friend, take turns reading from your chart. Together, see if you can think of some more uses for water to add to your charts.

Do You Know?

- All living things must have water to survive.

- Most people will drink about 16,000 gallons of water in a lifetime.

- More than two-thirds of the earth is covered with water.

- Almost all the water on the earth is in the oceans.

- About two-thirds of your body is made up of water.

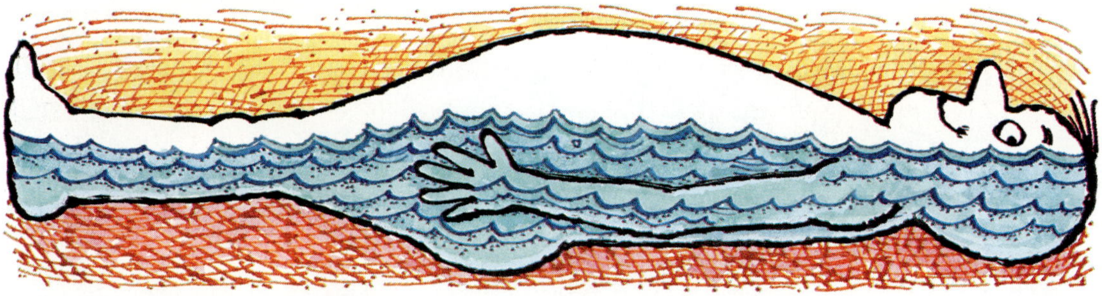

- About three-fourths of a chicken's body is made up of water.

The citizens plan to let only the most beautiful horses into their city. What will happen to change their minds?

Fritz and the Beautiful Horses

by Jan Brett

Once there was a walled city known for its beautiful horses. There were magnificent jumpers, splendid chargers, and elegant parade horses.

The citizens were so proud of these horses that they passed a law that allowed only the most beautiful horses into the city. All others had to stay outside. One of these was a pony named Fritz.

Fritz was not beautiful. He had a long, tangled mane, whiskers on his muzzle, and short legs. But Fritz was very gentle and kind. He was sure-footed and always willing to work.

Day after day, hour after hour, Fritz watched the beautiful horses. Some had braided manes and tails and carried lovely ladies. Others had glossy coats and pulled grand carriages. Most of all, he watched the children's horses.

"I wonder why the children look so frightened?" he thought.

The children were afraid. They didn't like their horses prancing and leaping. It made them very difficult to ride.

As Fritz watched he thought, "I would like a child to ride me." But no one ever noticed Fritz.

One day he climbed up to the road leading to the walled city. He tried to take long, graceful strides. He pranced and curved his neck. He threw his tail into the air. Fritz wanted to be noticed.

The citizens stared at Fritz and then they began to laugh. "Look at that silly horse," they said. "What a misfit!"

Then the lovely ladies and the magnificent gentlemen galloped away toward the walled city. The children followed reluctantly behind. "I guess I do look silly," thought Fritz, and he hung his head sadly.

Fritz listened as the citizens galloped their horses faster and faster. He heard their loud cheers as they rode onto the bridge to the walled city.

All of a sudden, he heard a loud *snap*. The bridge was breaking under the weight of the horses.

Fritz saw a large crack appear in the middle of the bridge. The citizens were on one side, and the children were on the other. "You'll have to cross through the river," cried the citizens.

But the children wouldn't move.

"My horse might shy and buck," said one.

"My horse might leap and stumble," said another.

"We might fall off," they all cried.

"Stay where you are," shouted the citizens. "We will come and get you." But their horses wouldn't move.

"This hill is much too steep," thought one horse.

"My lovely mane might get tangled in the bushes," thought another.

"We certainly don't want to get wet," all the horses agreed.

Everyone wondered what to do. Then they noticed Fritz.

Fritz was carefully climbing to where the children waited.

Fritz was not beautiful, but he was gentle and kind. He was sure-footed and always willing to work. The children were not afraid to ride him.

One by one, Fritz carried the children carefully down the steep hill. He calmly stepped through the river from rock to rock and up the other side.

In that way, he carried all the children to the walled city.

A great cheer went up from the citizens.

The lovely ladies cried, "Hooray for the sure-footed pony!"

The gentlemen said, "How kind and dependable he is! How sorry we are for misunderstanding him before."

So Fritz was given a special place in the walled city. All the children cared for him and became his friends.

From that day on, the walled city was known for its beautiful horses and its very dependable pony.

Discussing the Selection

1. Why did the citizens let Fritz into the city?
2. Why hadn't Fritz been allowed into the city at first?
3. How did Fritz carry the children to safety?
4. When in the story did you first know that Fritz would save the children?
5. What do you think the author was trying to tell you in this story?

Using Language

Writing Laws

Planning The citizens passed a law that allowed only the most beautiful horses into the city. What did you think of that law? Pretend that you have to make some laws for your school. What kinds of laws would you make?

Working Together Get together with a group of classmates. Make some laws for your school. Make sure that the laws you make are good ones and that your classmates can follow them. Have someone in your group write the laws you make.

Sharing Share the laws your group made with the class. The class may vote on whether or not each law should be passed. Write all the laws that are passed on a chart called *School Laws*.

UNIT CLOSER

MAKING PLANS

Each of the stories in this unit was about plans that were made and carried out. Tell what plans were made in each story and whether the plans worked out the way they were supposed to. Then answer the following questions:

1. When Ut first went to her new school, the other children made fun of her. But when her classmates grew to understand her, they became her friends. What other character in this unit was like Ut?

2. What are some things you learned about water in this unit?

3. Which characters from this unit could be described as thoughtful? What did these characters do that was thoughtful?

4. Fritz kept going back and forth across the river until all the children were saved. What other characters in this unit stuck with a plan until they got what they wanted?

Bibliography

Books in This Unit

Fritz and the Beautiful Horses by Jan Brett. Houghton Mifflin, 1981.

Why the Sun and the Moon Live in the Sky by Elphinstone Dayrell. Houghton Mifflin, 1968.

Children of the Yukon by Ted Harrison. Tundra, 1977.

Angel Child, Dragon Child by Michele Maria Surat. Raintree, 1983.

Additional Books to Read

Very Last, First Time by Jan Andrews. Atheneum, 1986.

Dr. DeSoto by William Steig. Farrar, Straus & Giroux, 1982.

Zoom at Sea by Tim Wynne-Jones. Groundwood, 1983.

BONUS

Pig and Duck want to visit Moose in the country. How does Moose suggest they get there?

A Weekend in the Country

by Lee Lorenz

It was the hottest day of the summer. The power had gone out the night before, and there was no ice, no air-conditioning, and no TV.

Pig and Duck sat behind drawn shades in their bathing suits, fanning themselves and trying to play cards.

“These cards keep sticking together,” said Duck grumpily.

“And this popcorn is soggy,” said Pig.

“What we need is a weekend in the country,” said Pig. “I’ll call Moose and ask him to invite us to his farm.”

"Come on up," said Moose, "and bring your fishing rods and your bathing suits. We'll have a great time!"

"Wonderful!" said Pig. "How do we get there?"

"Take the bus," replied Moose. "I think that's easiest."

"I *love* buses," said Pig. "The new ones are so big and fast!"

"And cool," added Duck. "We can relax and enjoy the view."

"I'll bet they serve snacks," said Pig.

"Hold on a moment," said Moose. "You'll have to take the local bus by way of Fidget's Folly. And be sure to bring your hip boots."

"Boots?" asked Pig and Duck together.

"It's been pretty muddy after the big storms, and you might have to help push the old bus up the hill," explained Moose.

"Where do we go from there?" asked Pig with caution.

"There's a connecting bus every three hours to Hunter's Notch," replied Moose. "By the way, if the driver's name is Ed Pilsner, take the next one. Ed fell asleep behind the wheel last month and drove right into the river. He had to be towed upstream.

"Oh, and don't forget your sleeping bags," added Moose.

"How come?" asked Pig.

"Sometimes the bus breaks down," said Moose. "If you got caught in the woods at night, you wouldn't want to try to walk out. Some mighty strange things happen around there after dark."

"Maybe the train would be better," suggested Pig quietly.

"Well, there are three a day from the city to Bear Creek," said Moose.

"I *love* trains," said Pig.

"Me, too," said Duck. "Thick, soft seats, air-conditioning. We can bring some books to read or play cards."

"And, of course, there's always the dining car," added Pig.

"This isn't one of those fancy trains," said Moose. "It's just two cars. Bring your own drinking water and don't forget a roll of mosquito netting."

"Mosquito netting?" asked Pig.

"There's a three-hour wait at Bear Creek," said Moose. "The station burned down last week, and the mosquitoes around there are as big as bluejays."

"What next?" asked Pig.

"Take the Spur Line to Potter's Corner. From there just follow the cow path right to my front door. Oh, and be sure to bring some flares."

"Why flares?" asked Pig.

"You might not get here before sundown," said Moose. "You wouldn't want to get lost out there with all those hungry bears around. If you have any problem just send up a flare, and the sheriff will be there in no time."

"That seems very complicated," said Pig. "Maybe we should come by boat."

"I *do* love the water," said Duck.

"It's nice and cool on a boat. Gentle breezes, deck chairs," he added.

"Tasty snacks," said Pig.

"I'm afraid they don't have a snack bar," said Moose, "but you could pack a lunch. And bring a rubber raft along just in case. The boat sprang a leak yesterday, and they barely made it to shore."

"On second thought . . ." began Pig.

"Don't worry," interrupted Moose. "You're never more than half a mile from land. A boat will come along and take you to Bestrop's logging camp. Get off there and float downstream on the logs to Herner's Canal. Stay to the left or you might go over the falls."

"And don't forget a bunch of carrots," Moose added.

"Carrots?" said Pig.

"When you get to the canal, you take the mule-drawn raft. Sometimes the mule gets stubborn, but a bunch of carrots will keep him going."

"I see," said Pig.

"I'll meet you at the end of the canal with the tractor. From there it's just eight miles across the fields to home."

"We only have a weekend," said Pig. "Maybe we should fly."

"You city people," laughed Moose. "Always in a hurry."

"I love flying," said Duck. "Comfortable seats, air-conditioning."

"And free meals," added Pig.

"This plane is a little different," interrupted Moose. "They carry mostly chickens and farm tools, but they can squeeze in some passengers.

"There are two flights a day to Purdy's Mills Farm. That's just down the road from me. Of course, the weather can be bad so bring a parachute."

"Parachute!" said Pig.

"A terrible thing happened here last month," Moose said. "A plane got caught in a storm, and they had to drop everything on it by parachute."

Pig and Duck looked at each other.

Just then the air-conditioning started humming. "The power's on!" cried Duck. "Ice, cool air, TV!"

"I just remembered," said Pig to Moose, "that my parachute is at the laundry."

"Mine, too," added Duck.

"Maybe we should come up another time," said Pig.

"Come to think of it," said Moose, "the dog just had puppies in the guest room. Why don't you call me next weekend?"

"I will," said Pig and hung up.

Pig and Duck made a big pitcher of lemonade. They turned the air-conditioner way up and played cards and watched TV. Outside it was as hot as ever, but inside it was nice and cool.

"This is nice," said Duck, "but it's nothing like a weekend in the country."

"It certainly isn't," said Pig with a smile. "Thank goodness!"

Glossary

The Glossary is a special dictionary that has definitions for some of the words used in this book. Following the definition of each word, there is a sentence in which the word is used.

A

ad·ven·ture A very unusual or thrilling experience: Visiting the fire station was a real *adventure*.

af·fect To have an effect upon: Rosa was *affected* by the sad story. **affected**

a·mong **1** In the group of: He was *among* the singers who entered the contest. **2** In pieces for each.

a·pron Something that is worn to protect clothing: We wear *aprons* whenever we are painting. **aprons**

ar·e·a **1** The amount or size of something: What is the *area* of this floor? **2** A place or section.

ar·rest To take to jail: The thief was *arrested*. **arrested**

at·tempt **1** To try: We will *attempt* to do the job in three days. **2** A try.

av·er·age Not good or bad; ordinary: It was an *average* winter day.

B

bam·boo A tall, treelike grass used for building and making things: I have a *bamboo* table.

ban·is·ter The railing on a staircase: We have a new *banister* for our front steps.

beau·ti·ful Lovely; nice to look at: This is a *beautiful* flower.

be·hav·ior The way a person or a thing acts: We are happy about his good *behavior*.

bold **1** Being able to meet danger or pain without being afraid: The *bold* soldier went to war. **2** Easily seen, as an outline or color.

bold·face A kind of printing in which the lines are thick and dark: The title was printed in *boldface*.

bon·net A hat that covers most of the hair and is held on with strings or ribbons tied under the chin: The baby is wearing a pink *bonnet*.

brag To talk too much about what one has, has done, or can do: They always *brag* about their big house.

Braille A way of printing in which the letters are shown by raised dots and are read by touching with the fingers: This book is written in *Braille*.

break **1** To separate or crack into pieces: He tried to *break* the branch off the tree. **2** To make or become useless.

bridge A structure built across something, on which cars, or other things cross over: The car went across the *bridge*.

brief Not long; short: Her visit was *brief*.

broad Large from side to side; wide: The *broad* table held all of the food.

built Having been made by putting parts or materials together: He *built* this house.

bur·ro A small donkey. The *burro* carried two packs of grain from the field.

bur·row **1** To hide or snuggle: Morty *burrowed* under his covers. **2** A hole made in the ground and lived in by certain animals. **burrowed**

bur·y To hide or keep from being seen: He *buried* the paper in his books. **buried**

C

ca·noe A small boat with a point at both ends, moved by paddles: We went down the river in a *canoe.*

car·riage A vehicle with two or more wheels, used for carrying people: The *carriages* were pulled by horses. **carriages**

cat·nap A short sleep: A baby takes a lot of *capnaps* during a day. **catnaps**

cau·tion Care to keep bad things from happening: Use *caution* when driving.

chant To say a group of words in such a way that it sounds like a song: The class will *chant* the poem.

cit·i·zen A person who is born in or who has formally declared his or her loyalty to a country: My family and I are *citizens* of the United States. **citizens**

clue A piece of information that helps to solve a problem or a mystery: Your *clues* helped us to solve the puzzle. **clues**

col·on A punctuation mark (:), used to introduce a long quotation, a number of things coming one after another, or an example: I used a *colon* in this definition.

com·plain To find or say that something is bad, wrong, or uncomfortable: I knew he would *complain* about the noise.

com·pli·cate Not simple or easy: The *complicated* directions were difficult to follow. **complicated**

con·fess To admit to having done something wrong: Meg *confessed* that she had not cleaned up the spilled milk. **confessed**

coun·try **1** The place where one is born: In my *country*, it snows a lot. **2** An open area of land.

crea·ture A living animal or person: This bird is the most beautiful *creature* I have ever seen.

cur·i·ous Wanting to know more: Dan is a *curious* boy.

curve A line that bends and has no straight parts: A *curve* is not a straight line.

D

daugh·ter What a girl is to her parents: The mother and her *daughter* look alike.

de·scrip·tion The words that tell about something: Martha gave a good *description* of her lost cat.

des·crip·tive Telling what a person or thing is like: His *descriptive* words told us just how she looked.

de·tec·tive A person, often a police officer, whose work is solving mysteries: The *detective* found a clue to the crime.

de·vour To eat up hungrily: Watch him as he *devours* that apple. **devours**

dis·a·gree·ment A difference of opinions; an argument: We had a *disagreement* about what time to leave.

dis·place To take the place of: When marbles are added to water, they *displace* the water at the bottom of the container.

dis·traught Very upset: She was *distraught* when she heard the bad news.

dough A soft mixture of flour, a liquid, and other things, used for making such foods as bread or biscuits: The baker put the *dough* in the pan.

dur·ing 1 Throughout the time of: The pool is open *during* the day. **2** While something else is going on.

E

egg·nog A drink made of eggs, milk, and sugar: We drink *eggnog* on special holidays.

eight One more than seven: I have *eight* books.

el·e·gant Beautiful: This is an *elegant* dress.

el·e·phant A large, four-legged mammal that has a long trunk, thick skin, and tusks: We saw an *elephant* at the zoo.

en·e·my A person or group who hates and tries to harm another: He stayed away from his *enemies*. **enemies**

ex·cuse To allow to leave: Elena asked if she could be *excused* from the table. **excused**

F

fan·ta·sy Something that is imagined: Beth has a *fantasy* that one day she will walk on the moon.

fa·vor A kind act: He did me a *favor* and picked up the book.

fee A price or charge for doing something: We had to pay a *fee* to play golf.

fes·ti·val A celebration that happens every year: We went to the spring flower *festival*.

fi·nal·ly At last; at the end: She *finally* finished the job.

fin·er·y Very good clothes or decorations: Everyone at the fancy party was dressed in their *finery*.

flare A bright light or fire used for signaling: The *flares* on the ground helped the pilot land the plane. **flares**

flock A large group: The *flock* of sheep move together.

folk Coming from or having to do with ordinary people: I like to sing *folk* songs.

fourth Next after the third: He is the *fourth* person in line.

fringe A border or outer edge: There is red *fringe* on this tablecloth.

G

gen·tly In a soft or kind way: Donna *gently* covered the sleeping child.

glare **1** To stare with anger or dislike: He *glared* at his enemy. **2** To give off a bright, blinding light. **glared**

gleam A light that shines for only a short time: I saw a *gleam* of light in the sky.

glos·sy Smooth and shiny: The top of this table is *glossy*.

grace·ful Moving in a very beautiful or delicate way: We watched the *graceful* dancer.

graph A chart that shows how two sets of information go together: This *graph* shows how much it has rained in each month this year.

grove A small group of trees: We had a picnic in the *grove*.

guess **1** To answer correctly: She *guessed* the answer to the riddle. **2** To make up one's mind without knowing enough to be sure. **guessed**

guest A person who is being entertained by someone else: I was a *guest* in her home.

H

half·way In the middle: This is the *halfway* point of the race.

help·less Not able to do things for oneself: The new baby was *helpless*.

hol·ler **1** To shout: She heard someone *holler* her name. **2** A shout.

hour The amount of time in any one of the twenty-four parts of a day: It takes an *hour* to get to Grandma's house.

hud·dle To crowd together closely: The birds *huddled* together in the cozy nest. **huddled**

hu·mor Words that make something funny or amusing: Her story was full of *humor*.

I

in·sist To stand up for one's beliefs: He *insisted* that he was right. **insisted**

in·ter·rupt To make someone or something stop what is being done by breaking in: The thunder *interrupted* my sleep. **interrupted**

i·ron **1** A very strong metal that is used for many things: The fence was made of *iron*. **2** An appliance used to press wrinkles out of clothes.

J

jeal·ous Wanting to have what someone else has: Pedro is *jealous* of Rita's new bike.

joy·ous Full of happiness: This is a *joyous* day.

L

let·tuce A plant with crisp, green leaves that are eaten: I put *lettuce* on my sandwich.

liq·uid Something that can be poured, as water or milk: Juice is a *liquid*.

lo·cal Having to do with one neighborhood or small area: This is the *local* grocery store.

lose To be unable to find something: Mother told her not to *lose* her mittens.

M

mane The long hair growing on and around the neck of an animal: A lion has a *mane*.

ma·te·ri·als The things needed for doing something: She has the *materials* that she needs to paint a picture.

med·al A small piece of metal with words or pictures on it, given as an award: She got a *medal* for winning the race.

min·ute A measurement of time made up of sixty seconds: My favorite program begins in one *minute*.

mis·fit Something or someone that does not fit in: She felt like a *misfit* when she was with the older children.

mo·ment A very short point in time: I'll be with you in just a *moment*.

month One of the twelve parts into which the year is divided: There are twelve *months* in a year. **months**

mos·qui·to A small flying insect, the female of which bites and sucks blood from people and animals: A *mosquito* bit me on the arm.

muk·luk A reindeerskin or sealskin boot or slipper: She wears *mukluks* to keep her feet warm. **mukluks**

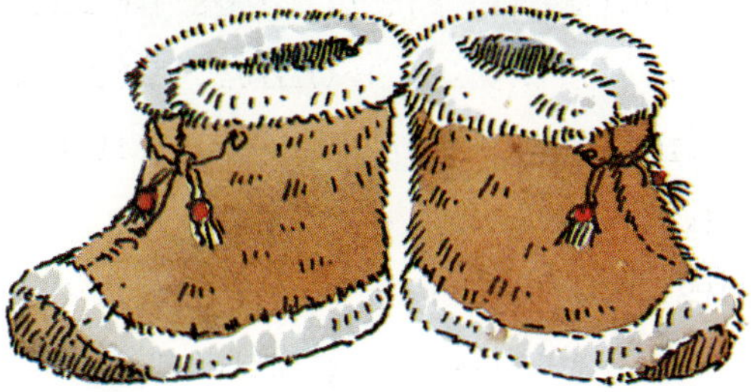

mu·sic A melodical series of sounds made by voices or instruments: There are many different kinds of *music* on the radio.

muz·zle A device put on the nose and mouth of an animal to stop the animal from barking or biting: That mean dog is wearing a *muzzle*.

N

naught 1 Nothing: After the fire she was left with *naught*. **2** The numeral 0; zero.

no·tice To see: I keep *noticing* wrong answers in my math homework. **noticing**

O

o·cean A great body of salt water that covers the earth: On our vacation, we swam in the *ocean*.

of·fice A place in which work is done: Bill moved into a bigger *office*.

om·e·let Eggs beaten together, cooked, and folded in half, sometimes with a filling: I ordered a cheese *omelet* for breakfast.

op·po·site Facing or moving the other way: The two cars were traveling in *opposite* directions.

ought To have a duty or a responsibility: I *ought* to go home and wash the windows.

ov·en The part of a stove used for baking and roasting: The cake is baking in the *oven*.

P

par·a·chute A large sheet of material, shaped like an umbrella, used for slowing a person or a thing down as it falls from high in the air: She jumped from the airplane and opened her *parachute*.

par·don To forgive: *Pardon* me for stepping on your foot.

pa·ren·the·ses The curved lines ( ), used to set off words or phrases: I put *parentheses* around the definition.

pas·sen·ger A person who rides in something, such as a bus or a plane: They were the last *passengers* to get on the train. **passengers**

piece A part of something separated from the whole: I ate one *piece* of the apple.

pre·fix Letters added to the beginning of a word to make a new word: We learned the *prefix un-* in class today.

prompt·ly In a quick way; right away: The waiter *promptly* brought us our food.

push To make a way through by force: The snowplow *pushes* its way through the snow. **pushes**

R

ra·ven A large, black bird: The *ravens* made a lot of noise. **ravens**

re·al·ize To understand: I *realized* what I had done wrong. **realized**

re·frig·er·a·tor A place where foods or other materials are kept fresh by cooling: The milk is in the *refrigerator*.

re·luc·tant·ly Not wanting to do something: She *reluctantly* left the picnic.

re·mark·a·ble Extraordinary; unusual; special: He did a *remarkable* job.

rust·y Covered with a reddish or dark brown coating that forms on iron or steel: The front of her bike was *rusty*.

S

sand-col·ored Having a tan or brownish color like the color of sand: The *sand-colored* bird blended in with the ground.

sat·is·fy 1 To give what is wanted or needed: The juice *satisfied* his thirst. **2** To free from worry. **satisfied**

sci·en·tist A person who does experiments and studies what things are made of: The *scientists* discovered a new planet. **scientists**

se·cret Something not to be told: She wouldn't tell her *secret* to anyone.

sel·dom Not often: I *seldom* walk down this street.

sense Clear or very easily understandable: The game directions made *sense* to me.

sew To make, fix, or put something together by using a needle and thread: I had to *sew* a button on my shirt.

since During the time after: We have not gone to the beach *since* summer.

sit·u·a·tion The way things are at a certain time or place: Police officers must deal with a lot of different *situations*. **situations**

skid To slide sideways: The car *skidded* on the ice. **skidded**

slith·er To slide down or along something with a side-to-side movement: The rattlesnake *slithered* down the rocky hill. **slithered**

sog·gy Filled with water or other liquid: The sauce made the bread *soggy*.

stub·born Not giving in easily: The *stubborn* mule wouldn't move.

stun To make unable to act: I was *stunned* when the ball hit me. **stunned**

sug·ar·cane A tall grass with a solid stalk that contains sugar: *Sugarcane* grows only where the weather is very warm.

sur·vive 1 To live through: He was able to *survive* the cold winter. **2** To live longer than someone else.

swal·low To make a motion that makes something go from the mouth into the stomach: Before speaking, I *swallowed* the food in my mouth. **swallowed**

swat·ter Something used to give a quick, sharp hit: I brought my *swatter* to the picnic in case there were flies.

T

tai·lor A person who makes or fixes clothes: I had a *tailor* shorten my pants.

through·out All during the time of: He slept *throughout* the concert.

tick-tack-toe A game in which players take turns placing X's and O's in a grid, trying to get three in a row: Max won the *tick-tack-toe* contest.

tight Fitting closely together: The players formed a *tight* huddle.

touch To come together; to be in contact with: Whoever *touches* the fence first wins. **touches**

trou·sers Pants: I have a pair of brown *trousers*.

tur·key A large bird that is used as food: We had *turkey* for Thanksgiving dinner.

U

u·nit·ed Joined together into one: The mayor listened to the *united* citizens' cries for more stoplights.

u·su·al·ly In a regular or normal way: He is *usually* on time for baseball practice.

V

vi·o·lin A musical instrument with four strings: The music from a *violin* is beautiful.

W

wel·come To greet gladly; to receive with joy: Pam and Alan *welcomed* us into their home. **welcomed**

whis·tle To make a shrill, high-pitched sound by pushing breath through the lips: She is *whistling* her favorite song. **whistling**

whole All of the parts that make up something: The *whole* class was in the play.

wil·der·ness An area of land that has not been cleared of its growth and has no one living on it: There are many animals in the *wilderness*.

wits The ability to understand: He is a person of quick *wits*.

work·shop A group of people who work on or study something together: I wrote a story to read in my writing *workshop*.

worth·while Something that is important enough to be done: This is a *worthwhile* movie to see.

Y

yam A kind of sweet potato: We ate *yams* with our turkey. **yams**

young Not old: The *young* children went to the early movie.

Acknowledgments (continued from page ii)

Macmillan Publishing Company: Adaptation of *Gregory, the Terrible Eater* by Mitchell Sharmat. Illustrations by Jose Aruego and Ariane Dewey. Text copyright © 1980 by Mitchell Sharmat. Illustrations copyright © 1980 by Jose Aruego and Ariane Dewey.

Gina Maccoby Literary Agency: "Uncles" from *Nuts to You, Nuts to Me* by Mary Ann Hoberman. Copyright © 1974 by Mary Ann Hoberman.

Carol Mann Literary Agency: "My Friend William Moved Away" by Martha Whitmore Hickman. Copyright © 1979 by Martha Whitmore Hickman.

Mary O'Neill: "Mimi's Fingers" from *Fingers Are Always Bringing Me News* by Mary O'Neill. Copyright © 1969 by Doubleday & Company, Inc.

Philomel Books: "Eskimo Chant" from *BEYOND THE HIGH HILLS, A Book of Eskimo Poems* translated by Knud Rasmussen. Copyright © 1961 by The World Publishing Company.

Plays, Inc.: "Finn McCool" by May Lynch from *Dramatized Folk Tales of the World* edited by Sylvia E. Kamerman. Copyright © 1967, 1971 by Plays, Inc.

Prentice-Hall, Inc.: From the book *A Weekend in the Country* written and illustrated by Lee Lorenz. Copyright © 1985 by Lee Lorenz.

Rourke Enterprises, Inc.: Jokes from *Sports Jokes* by Gary Chmielewski. Copyright © 1986 by Rourke Enterprises.

Scholastic Inc.: "The Story of Spray" from *Nine True Dolphin Stories* by Margaret Davidson. Text copyright © 1974 by Margaret Davidson.

Charles Scribner's Sons, a division of Macmillan, Inc.: Adaptation of *Josefina February* written and illustrated by Evaline Ness. Copyright © 1963 by Evaline Ness.

Larry Sternig Literary Agency: Adapted from *Misunderstood Animals* (retitled: "The Surprising Octopus") by Alice L. Hopf. Copyright © 1973 by Alice L. Hopf.

Tundra Books: Text and illustrations from *Children of the Yukon* by Ted Harrison. Copyright © 1977 by Ted Harrison.

Barbara K. Walker: Adaptation of *New Patches for Old* by Barbara K. Walker and Ahmet E. Uysal. Copyright © 1974 by Barbara K. Walker.

Illustrators
Liz Callen: 17, 164-165, 239; Rae Ecklund: 204-205, 206, 207, 209, 210, 212, 213, 214; Lois Ehlert: 226-227; Matt Faulkner: 199; Susan Jaekel: 122-123, 124, 126, 127, 129, 131, 132; Susan Lexa: 4, 6, 7, 8, 10, 11, 72-73, 75, 76, 77, 78; Don Madden: 156-157, 252-253; Ed Parker: 178-179, 180, 182, 183, 184, 187, 188-189, 190, 191, 193, 194, 195, 196; Diane Paterson: 83, 84, 85, 86, 88, 89, 92, 93, 94, 97, 284-295; Judith Sutton: 40, 41, 42, 43, 44, 46, 47, 48; Arieh Zeldich: 241, 242, 243, 244.

Photographs
2, Gabe Palmer/The Stock Market; 26-27, Laura Riley/Bruce Coleman; 29, 30, 32, Marineland Florida; 31, Lawrence Migdale/Photo Researchers; 67, H. Armstrong Roberts; 70, Joe Sachs; 80-81, Michal Heron; 100, 101, 102, 104, Rick Browne; 107, E.R. Degginger/Bruce Coleman; 136, Vicki Beller-Smith; 159, Jane Burton/Bruce Coleman; 160, Breck Kent/Animals, Animals; 161, 162, Oxford Scientific Films, G.I. Bernard/Animals, Animals; 202, Richard Haynes; 247, 248, John Lei/OPC.

Cover Photograph: Roger Tory Peterson/Photo Researchers

Design and Production: Kirchoff/Wohlberg, Inc.